WILD IRISH LOVE

Praise for other books by Marian Broderick

BOLD, BRILLIANT & BAD
'A delicious directory of fascinating Irish women …
their stories tower'
The Irish Times

'Astonishing, true-life stories of audacious dames!'
Midwest Book Review

WILD IRISH WOMEN
'A rollicking read'
Books Ireland

'After reading this book, one can never again
ignore the role of Irishwomen'
Dublin Historical Record

'Broderick's prose is simple and accessible, and her
fascination with her two favourite subjects –
Irish history and women's studies
– jumps out from every page'
Sunday Business Post

Marian Broderick is a writer and editor who lives and works in London. She is second-generation Irish; her parents are from Donegal and Limerick. She spent every summer of her childhood in Ireland and has developed strong links with the place and the people. *Wild Irish Women: Extraordinary Lives from History* proved hugely popular on publication in 2001 and Marian furthered her research to bring the reader more wild Irish women in *Bold, Brilliant & Bad: Irish Women from History* (2018).

WILD IRISH LOVE

Great Romances from History

Marian Broderick

THE O'BRIEN PRESS
DUBLIN

First published 2021 by
The O'Brien Press Ltd,
12 Terenure Road East,
Rathgar, Dublin 6,
D06 HD27,
Ireland.
Tel: +353 1 4923333; Fax: +353 1 4922777
E-mail: books@obrien.ie; Website: obrien.ie
The O'Brien Press is a member of Publishing Ireland.

ISBN: 978–1-78849-182-2

1 3 5 7 9 10 8 6 4 2
21 23 25 24 22

Front cover image: Jean Reutlinger (1875–1917) Wikimedia Commons;
Back cover image: Library of Congress;

Printed and bound in Poland by Białostockie Zakłady Graficzne S.A.
The paper in this book is produced using pulp from managed forests.

Published in:

DUBLIN
UNESCO
City of Literature

Dedication

To Alfredo Cristiano with love

Acknowledgements

Thanks to Conall for all the cups of tea over the last year. Gratitude to my sister and first reader, Liz Cormack, for incisive and helpful comment. Thanks to Aileen and David Norton for extra design and editorial advice. Thanks to Susan Houlden for eagle-eyed editing, Emma Byrne for beautiful design and Michael O'Brien for good ideas.

A first edition of *Ulysses*, banned in several countries, including the UK and USA.

CONTENTS

Legendary Lovers

Secrets & Scandals

When Love Goes Wrong

Love Fast, Die Young

Inspirations

At the touch of love everyone

becomes a poet.

Plato

From the earthy sensuality of James Joyce's
Molly Bloom to the witty irreverence of
George Bernard Shaw's Eliza Doolittle,
creative natures have always yearned to
immortalise their loved ones.

Maud Gonne, *c.* 1901.

Maud Gonne & WB Yeats

I have spread my dreams under your feet;
Tread softly because you tread on my dreams.

WB Yeats, 'He Wishes for the Cloths of Heaven' (1899)

When WB Yeats and Maud Gonne first met in a sedate London drawing room, they instantly knew their destinies were entwined. The fates of Ireland's greatest poet and one of its greatest romantic heroines were to be linked for forty years; they were more than friends or lovers, they were soulmates.

They met in the well-corseted Victorian manner, via a polite letter of introduction, in the Yeats family home. With masses of red-gold hair and fiery amber eyes, Maud, aged twenty-two, was about to hit the Irish nationalist scene. Tall and lanky with glasses and a floppy fringe, Willie, as Maud called him, was, at twenty-three, already dreaming up the Irish Literary Revival.

The two bonded over their love of Ireland and their plans for its bright future. She wanted nothing less than a revolution, excising British influence in Ireland and achieving full independence by force. He wanted a renaissance of Gaelic culture, language and customs. Their passions coincided, not to mention the fact that

Maud was so beautiful that she seemed, Willie later wrote, 'of a divine race'. By the time the minutes of that first social call had ticked away, 'the troubling' of his life had begun.

They met often and wrote letters incessantly. The charismatic Maud became a celebrity as she toured Ireland, speaking out about evicted tenants, starving children and brutalised prisoners. Willie developed as a poet and dramatist, pouring his love for Maud and his vision of the Celtic Twilight into his work. They affected each other deeply. Under Maud's influence, Willie briefly joined the Irish Republican Brotherhood (the IRB, the secret forerunner of the IRA, Irish Republican Army). Under Willie's influence, Maud acted in plays and joined the Order of the Golden Dawn, a secret society devoted to the occult.

But in the deadly phrase all too familiar to many a frustrated young man, Maud loved her beloved Willie 'as a friend'. She was all for their idyllic spiritual connection to grow ever deeper, but Willie was a red-blooded male – he yearned for a physical one too. He made the first of many proposals of marriage in 1891. Maud – wisely, as it turned out – said no.

> ... you make beautiful poetry out of what you call your unhappiness and you are happy in that. Marriage would be such a dull affair. Poets should never marry. The world should thank me for not marrying you.
>
> Letter from Maud to Willie in 1914

Maud's golden eyes, her creamy skin and her regal walk haunted Willie. Always just out of reach, she appeared in dozens of his poems. In 'A Second Troy' she was Helen, unable to help the devastated hearts she left in her wake. In 'Friends' she 'took all / Till my youth was gone / With scarce a pitying look'.

But the aloof Maud had been keeping secrets from Willie. In the first five years of their friendship, she secretly gave birth to two children by her married French lover, Lucien Millevoye. Grief-stricken when her first baby, a son, died, she became fixated on the possibilities of reincarnation. She then deliberately conceived a second baby near his tomb, and passed this child off as her ward. Thus, even as the rumours swirled, appearances were maintained. Money cushioned Maud against a world whose scorn would have ruined her.

All this and more did Maud reveal to Willie in 1898, when her relationship with Millevoye broke down. Shocked to his very soul as he was, the revelation did not weaken Yeats's feelings for her. Quite the opposite – Willie loved the vulnerable, shattered Maud even more than the queenly beauty. He redoubled his efforts to persuade her to marry him. He proposed repeatedly; he was rejected repeatedly.

In truth, why should Maud have married Willie? Though they were suited in many ways, there were important exceptions. She was wealthy; he was relatively poor. He was a proud Protestant all his life; and she was on a spiritual journey to Catholicism. She thought violence was part of the Irish independence struggle; he abhorred it. He needed physical love; she had a fear of sex. He wanted a wife and home; she was nomadic and unsuited to domesticity.

So Willie was understandably devastated when, in 1903, he found out that Maud was getting married. The groom was soldier and revolutionary Major John MacBride. In a 1904 poem, 'Never Give all the Heart', an anguished Willie advises other young men not to render themselves 'deaf, dumb and blind with love', as he has.

Despite now becoming part of a nationalist power couple with MacBride, it seems Maud had been right all along – the only marriage she was suited for was the 'mystical marriage' she shared with Willie. She left MacBride and moved to France, but the bond between her and Willie held firm over the miles. They had always shared a belief in the supernatural and the occult, and now were drawn in even deeper. Maud claimed the power of astral travel and visited Willie in her dreams.

In 1908 in Paris, they finally consummated their affair and slept together. It had taken nearly twenty years to get to this point and it should have been decisive. But, perhaps not so surprisingly, the development did not lead to their happy-ever-after. Maud's subsequent letter informed Willie that she was praying to 'have all earthly desire taken from my love for you'. She hoped that his desire for her would evaporate too.

In 1916 Maud was widowed when MacBride was executed for his part in the Easter Rising. Willie travelled to France and asked her to marry him one more time, more it seems out of habit than hope. Maud yet again declined, whereupon he proposed to

WB Yeats, *c.* 1903.

her daughter, Iseult. She too declined. Willie, desperate to make a proper home at Thoor Ballylee in Galway and determined to marry someone, returned to Ireland and proposed to twenty-five-year-old Georgie Hyde-Lees, who accepted. He never had cause to regret it; Georgie was an intelligent, competent young woman who recognised her husband's genius, collaborated with him creatively, and made his dank, remote castle habitable. Maud never remarried and wore black in memory of her estranged husband's death. She and Willie remained friends.

﹏ Happy ever after? ﹏

While Willie became a cornerstone of the new Irish Free State in the 1920s and '30s, Maud's unswerving republicanism made her a thorn in the side of successive governments. While he revelled in his place in the literary and political establishment, Maud founded the WPDL (Women's Prisoners' Defence League) and remained a hunger-striking, prison-going radical. When she was arrested in 1918 and 1923, Yeats lobbied to have her released.

Perhaps there are different forms of a happy ending. Maud once told Willie that the world would thank her for not marrying him because of the beautiful poetry he created out of his love for her. She was right. Without his love for her, the world would not have had poems such as 'He Wishes for the Cloth of Heaven', 'The Pity of Love', 'When You are Old', 'The Folly of Being Comforted', 'Adam's Curse', 'Old Memory', 'A Poet to his Beloved', 'A Woman Homer Sung', 'Reconciliation', 'No Second Troy', and many others. But she and Willie were so much more than poet and muse. They were legends in their own lifetime.

No Second Troy

Why should I blame her that she filled my days

With misery, or that she would of late

Have taught to ignorant men most violent ways,

Or hurled the little streets upon the great,

Had they but courage equal to desire?

What could have made her peaceful with a mind

That nobleness made simple as a fire,

With beauty like a tightened bow, a kind

That is not natural in an age like this,

Being high and solitary and most stern?

Why, what could she have done, being what she is?

Was there another Troy for her to burn?

Timeline

13 June 1865 William Butler Yeats born Sandymount, Dublin, Ireland

21 December 1866 Edith Maud Gonne born Tongham, Surrey, England

1889 Maud visits the Yeats home and meets the man she called Willie

1890 Maud's son Georges born (dies aged eighteen months)

1894 Maud's daughter Iseult Gonne born

1902 Maud takes title role in Yeats's play *Cathleen Ni Houlihan*

1903 Maud marries Major John MacBride in Paris; they separate the following year

1904 Maud's son Seán MacBride born

1917 Willie marries Georgie Hyde-Lees in a London registry office; they have two children

1918 Maud goes on hunger strike while interned in Holloway Prison, London

1922 Willie appointed to brand-new Irish Senate

1923 Maud imprisoned by the Irish Free State for sedition; Willie awarded Nobel Prize for Literature

28 January 1939 Willie dies, Hôtel Idéal Séjour in Menton, France; eventually buried in Sligo

27 April 1953 Maud dies, Clonskeagh, Dublin; buried in Republican Plot, Glasnevin Cemetery, Dublin

James Joyce, *c.* 1930s.

James Joyce & Nora Barnacle

His heart danced upon her movements like a cork upon a tide.

James Joyce, *A Portrait of the Artist as a Young Man* (1916)

There are good first dates and bad first dates – and then there are those that go down in history. When James Joyce took Nora Barnacle for a walk on 16 June 1904, it was such a profound experience for them both that it changed their lives beyond recognition, and was immortalised in fiction.

Nora was a good-looking twenty-year-old from Galway city when she bumped into James on Nassau Street, Dublin, one sunny June day. She had recently absconded from her home in Galway and was working as a chambermaid and waitress in nearby Finn's Hotel. Twenty-two-year-old James was supposed to be working as a book reviewer, but instead was drinking and debauching his way around Dublin city. They were introduced by a mutual friend.

When Nora met James, she didn't think much of him. He looked like a Swedish sailor on shore leave with his battered yachting cap, threadbare trousers and the tattiest tennis shoes she'd ever seen. He was handsome but unhappy, with no money, no publisher for his work and no permanent home. He was on a downward spiral, regularly drowning his sorrows and frequenting brothels. His only asset was a rock-solid confidence in his own genius, which no-one else shared.

But when James met Nora, he liked what he saw very much indeed. Nora was tall, with masses of auburn hair and a beautiful west of Ireland accent. She had a slight squint in one eye, which made her look sleepy and sexy. She was bright, funny and, as he would very soon discover, sensual. He wasted no time in asking her to go out with him.

They arranged to meet in Merrion Square – but on this first occasion Nora didn't show up. Maybe she'd had second thoughts about getting involved with this well-spoken jackeen with the raggedy clothes, or maybe she simply had to work. Whatever the reason, James persevered. He wrote the first of what would turn out, over the years, to be hundreds of letters to Nora. He admitted he was so short-sighted that even if she had turned up he might well have missed her. Nora wrote back agreeing to meet him the following evening, 16 June.

This day is still celebrated by Joyce-lovers in Dublin as Bloomsday, but even the biggest Joyce fan couldn't describe the original outing as glamorous. James and Nora hadn't a bean between them, so their first date consisted, not of dinner or dancing, but a four-kilometre (two-and-a-half mile) trek through the rough eastern suburb of Ringsend to Sandymount Strand. Love may not have been in the air just yet, but lust certainly was; their sexual chemistry was sizzling and, once they were in the sand dunes, things got physical. This was incredibly forward behaviour, and all the more remarkable because it was Nora who took the lead – and not for the last time in their relationship.

> … first I put my arms around him yes and drew him down to me so he could feel my breasts all perfume yes and his heart was going like mad and yes I said yes I will Yes.
>
> Molly Bloom, in James Joyce's *Ulysses*

Over the summer, they found they had much in common. Both had incorrigible alcoholic fathers and a fractured upbringing. (John Joyce had managed to waste a large inheritance, plunging his family of ten into poverty, while Tom Barnacle had abandoned his family of seven.) Both were sent away from home as children: James to boarding school, and Nora to her grandmother's house. Neither had much desire to spend time with their families.

Nora Barnacle Joyce,
c. 1915.

Both were inclined to flout social norms and challenge convention. James was courteous and kind, but to genteel Irish society his uncompromising honesty made him seem rude. He publicly despised his Catholic upbringing and the Church itself, which in turn despised him back. He hated conventions, such as marriage and baptism. His writing was incomprehensible to many and condemned as obscene.

As for Nora, she too had an unconventional streak. As a teenager, she used to steal men's clothes and go out in them. She also dated a Protestant, which was enough to earn her the beating from her uncle that made her run away. While the young James Joyce railed against the narrowness of Irish society, the young Nora Barnacle simply refused to be trapped in the life into which she'd been born.

Many people, both at the time and since, were snobbish about Nora's background, particularly her lack of education, the implication being that the girl who left school at twelve years old couldn't communicate with a University College Dublin graduate. Of course, it was nonsense. Nora was highly intelligent and entertaining – she and James never stopped talking. Whereas James was frightened of many things, including thunder, dogs and machinery, Nora feared nothing. Whereas he held grudges, she forgave in an instant. She wasn't one bit dazzled by the genius she called 'simple-minded Jim'.

> The thought of having to write ... what I would wish to speak were you beside me makes me utterly miserable ....
>
> Letter from Nora to James (1904)

By the end of summer 1904, James was obsessing about leaving Ireland for Europe. Nora again took the lead, telling him that if he was going, so was she. James, at first incredulous, slowly came round to the idea because, not only was he in lustful love with Nora, but she'd become essential to his peace of mind. He recognised that she would be his rock, his safe place in a chaotic world, his 'little bit of Ireland'. He was proud to take responsibility for her, but he was also honest. He told her there would be no wedding ring, no nice house and not much money. He was a writer, first and foremost, and would stay a writer. As long as she was able to accept these conditions, they'd be happy. Nora accepted.

Leaving her hotel job and accommodation was brave. Nora would have known many a song and story about what happened to unmarried women as soon as a baby was on the way. But she loved James and trusted him – and if she needed to get out of her humdrum existence with its claustrophobic future, he was the man to help her. Her wild side was ready for a leap into the unknown.

On 9 October 1904, having scrounged the fares, Nora and James boarded a ship bound for Liverpool en route to Paris, and set sail for their new life. Joyce Senior, tearfully waving his favourite child off from the North Wall, Dublin, was unaware that James had taken Nora with him – the two had boarded separately, to avoid gossip. Nora didn't even tell her family that she was leaving Ireland – and when she did write, she omitted to mention that she wasn't married. Despite the inauspicious start, Nora and James were to remain partners and soulmates for the rest of their lives.

Over the next thirty-seven years, Nora and James lived in rented flats in Trieste, Rome, Zurich and Paris. While James worked as a teacher and struggled to get published, Nora took in laundry to help support them. Just over nine months after setting sail from Dublin, Nora gave birth to a son, Georgio, followed two years later by a daughter, Lucia. The Joyces never had a penny, but made friends wherever they went (apart from landladies and other creditors), and became renowned as warm, very Irish hosts. They loved the high life, eating out every night, and visiting the opera. In 1912 Nora donned a fake wedding ring and visited Ireland with her children to patch things up with her family.

When James eventually published his seminal works *Ulysses* (1922) and *Finnegans Wake* (1939) he achieved great fame – or notoriety, depending on the point of view. The books were banned in many countries and had to be smuggled through customs in brown paper packages. Nora continued to put James and his work first all her life. It is now widely acknowledged that if it were not for her love and influence, James Joyce would have succumbed to alcoholism, just like his father.

In time James caved in on the subject of marriage so that Nora could have financial security in the event of his death. He and Nora were wed in London in 1931, twenty-six years after that first date in Sandymount. Ten years later, James died in Zurich of a perforated ulcer, and ten years after that, Nora died in Zurich of renal failure. The two are buried in Fluntern Cemetery, Zurich.

Today some of the most memorable women in fiction owe their existence to this fruitful relationship. In 'The Dead' from *Dubliners*, Gretta Conroy is based on Nora, as is Bertha in Joyce's only play *Exiles*. One of the most famous passages in literature, the soliloquy of sensual, mysterious, powerful Molly Bloom in the final episode of *Ulysses*, is a loving homage by James Joyce to Nora Barnacle Joyce.

Timeline

2 February 1882 James Augustine Aloysius Joyce born Rathgar, Dublin, Ireland

21 March 1884 Nora Joseph Barnacle born Galway Workhouse, Ireland

June 1904 James and Nora meet; 'Bloomsday'

October 1904 James and Nora leave Ireland

1905 Son Giorgio Joyce born

1907 Daughter Lucia Joyce born

1912 James and Nora's last visit to Ireland

1914 *Dubliners* published

1916 *A Portrait of the Artist as a Young Man* published

1922 *Ulysses* published

1939 *Finnegans Wake* published

4 July 1931 James and Nora marry

13 January 1941 James dies Zurich, Switzerland

10 April 1951 Nora dies Zurich, Switzerland

Molly Allgood, *c.* 1920s.

Molly Allgood & JM Synge

[A]ny girl would walk her heart out before she'd meet a young man was your like for eloquence, or talk, at all.

JM Synge, *The Playboy of the Western World* (1907)

She was a shop assistant turned actress, he was a posh, dying playwright, but Molly Allgood and John Millington Synge managed to bridge the huge gulf between them, and filled the short time they had together with life, love and creativity.

Their personalities couldn't have been more different. John was an intense, moody thirty-four-year-old, deeply absorbed in his craft, and Molly was a vivacious, daring eighteen-year-old, deeply absorbed in having a good time. Hailing from the Liberties in Dublin, all Molly had to her name was drive and talent. When her older sister Sara joined the Abbey Theatre and became its leading lady, Molly grabbed the chance to follow her, even though at first it meant languishing in her big sister's shadow. Her first part was a walk-on in John's third play, *The Well of the Saints*.

John had had a privileged life, but it hadn't shielded him from trouble. He'd had a string of broken love affairs, was battling a mysterious illness that came and went, and his provocative dramatic offerings at the Abbey generally met with booing and hissing due to their uncompromising non-propagandist content.

To Yeats's and Lady Gregory's dismay, when John met Molly, he was utterly captivated. Molly had bags of sex appeal, and a beautiful speaking voice, which was important to the dramatist with the musical ear. She was feisty, forthright and funny, with an energy that he often lacked. To Molly, John was impressive: poetic, sophisticated, European. His hollow cheeks made him handsome too – Molly had no idea that they meant he was a sick man.

Predictably enough, the Synge family came out against the fledgling love affair. The sixteen-year age gap didn't matter much to anybody – after all, maturity was a good thing in a man – but class and religion mattered a lot. John was from Anglo-Irish gentry, and a co-director of the Abbey. It was unseemly that he would even mix with cast members, let alone start courting one, and especially someone like Molly, who was penniless and Catholic.

As for the Allgoods, they also opposed the match, but on religious grounds. It was bad enough that John had started life as a Protestant, but now he was a full-blown atheist. His troublesome plays upset every good Catholic nationalist and showed the clergy in the poorest light. The career-minded Sara Allgood, perhaps a tiny bit put out at the potential elevation of her little sister to playwright's muse, sided with the naysayers over Molly's love affair. Soon they were speaking to each other only onstage.

The ensuing rows in the Synge and Allgood households forced John to move out of his mother's house and into private lodgings,

JM Synge, *c.* 1905.

and Molly to move out of her mother's and into her married sister's home.

Molly didn't care two straws what people said. She was in love for the first time with an influential man who could do her nothing but good. And John didn't care either. The mercurial Molly was fascinating, like a heroine in one of his plays – and pretty soon she would fulfil that role.

The relationship was not without its own drama. Letters flew between the Tramp and his Changeling, as they called themselves, full of lovers' tiffs and making up (John's side of the correspondence has been collected in *Letters to Molly*, edited by Ann Saddlemyer). When he was unwell, John was moody and often jealous of Molly out enjoying herself, while Molly could be defensive and impatient with his suspicions. When he was well, nature-loving John took the city girl on long walks in the hills of Wicklow where they thrashed out their differences. Soon, still against everyone's wishes, they announced their engagement and started to make plans for their wedding.

In 1906 John took the company on tour with *The Shadow of the Glen*, in which Molly had now moved from bit part to lead role. He also finished what would become his most famous work, *The Playboy of the Western World*.

In this comic masterpiece, Molly took the leading role of passionate, mercurial Pegeen Mike, a character that John based in part on her personality. The violence, the drinking, plus the risqué depiction of non-idealised, flesh-and-blood Irishwomen was hated on sight by an audience who yearned for a pure, unsullied national myth to help them through those troubled times. *Playboy* was felt to cast a slur on all Irish people, and Irishwomen in particular. Rioting duly ensued both inside and outside the Abbey on the first run. An ill John took to his bed, Yeats called the police but Molly acted on, unfazed though entirely inaudible through loud heckling in the native tongue. She knew a good part when she saw it; Pegeen Mike was the role of a lifetime and would make Molly's name.

Other than the *Playboy* riots, which lasted a week, 1907 constituted the pinnacle of John and Molly's happiness: outside Ireland, he was lauded as a major dramatic talent, she was a leading lady at last and they were busy buying furniture for their future home. In July, they spent a wonderful fortnight on holiday in Wicklow – in separate cottages, of course.

That fortnight was to stand for the honeymoon they were never to enjoy. John had, for the previous eight years, unknowingly been in the grip of a lymphatic cancer known as Hodgkins Disease, which now returned with a vengeance, swelling his neck glands and causing immense pain. Surgery in the spring of 1908 revealed that it was terminal. It would only be a matter of months. By the summer, John had moved back in with his mother. He wrote heart-breaking letters to Molly about storing away their new furniture. As autumn drew on, all talk of weddings quietly ceased.

[M]y heart's scalded this day, and I going off stretching out the earth between us, the way I'll not be waking near you another dawn of the year till the two of us do arise to hope or judgment with the saints of God.

Christy Mahon in *The Playboy of the Western World*

To get him through his last winter, John worked on turning the fable Deirdre of the Sorrows into a play. On her frequent visits, Molly encouraged him. He never finished it, for he was dead before the spring came.

Happy ever after?

Molly was just twenty-three when her dream future with John shattered. Because what she shared with John was regarded as somehow unsuitable, Molly was airbrushed out of his life. She did not attend his funeral, and her letters to him were destroyed, probably by his family. But she was a trouper, determined to carry on. She helped Yeats to finish Deirdre, then starred in it as the eponymous tragic heroine. The keening lament she produced nightly over her dead lover brought audience members to tears.

> But who'll pity Deirdre has lost the lips of Naisi [sic] from her neck and from her cheek forever? Who'll pity Deirdre has lost the twilight in the woods with Naisi, when beech trees were silver and copper and ash trees were fine gold?
>
> Molly Allgood (aka Máire O'Neill) in *Deirdre of the Sorrows*

Molly remained in high demand as a stage, film and radio actress her whole life, particularly in later years by the playwright Sean O'Casey. Her personal life, however, continued to be full of incident, some catastrophic. Having found love again in a happy marriage to a drama critic, she was widowed at the age of forty. She then rebounded into a brief ill-advised marriage to an old actor friend, which ended in divorce. She lost her son, named John after her dead fiancé, during World War II, and she struggled for years with alcoholism. Through it all, she continued to work.

In an ending as dramatic as any her first love could have written, Molly Allgood fell into a fireplace in her London lodgings after a long day working on one of her signature roles, Maisie Madigan from *The Silver Tassie* by Sean O'Casey. She died later in hospital of burns.

Timeline

16 April 1871 John Millington Synge born, Rathfarnham, Dublin

11 January 1886 Mary 'Molly' Allgood born, Mary St, Dublin

1896 Molly's father dies, and she and Sara spend time in an orphanage

1902 John co-founds the Irish National Theatre (later the Abbey) with WB Yeats and Lady Gregory

1903 Molly joins Maud Gonne's republican organisation Inghinidhe na hÉireann (Daughters of Ireland)

1903 *The Shadow of the Glen* staged

1904 *Riders to the Sea* staged

1905 Molly changes her stage name to Máire O'Neill

1907 *The Playboy of the Western World* staged; riots ensue

24 March 1909 John dies in Dublin, leaving *Deirdre of the Sorrows* drafted but unfinished

1911 Molly marries GH Mair, a drama critic, and has two children, Pegeen and John

1914 Molly makes New York debut in *General John Regan*

1930 Molly appears, with Sara, in Hitchcock's film of O'Casey's *Juno and the Paycock*

2 November 1952 Molly dies, Basingstoke, England

George Bernard Shaw, *c.* 1909, the year his plays were censored for blasphemy.

George Bernard Shaw & Stella Tanner

I want my rapscallionly fellow vagabond. I want my dark lady.

I want my angel – I want my tempter.

Letter from GBS to Stella (1913)

Bearded contrarian George Bernard Shaw, the world's greatest playwright (according to himself), was an unlikely ladies' man. Yet in middle age, he developed a habit of falling in love with talented actresses. Possibly the most beautiful and bewitching of them all was Stella Tanner, known professionally as Mrs Patrick Campbell.

> [Mrs Pat is] a dangerous woman for any man to set his affections on – a Deirdre to set men's hearts aflame!
>
> Reviewer Joseph Holloway on seeing
> Stella in the part of Yeats's *Deirdre*

It was a curiously delayed business. GBS and Stella, as they were known informally, had been acquainted for over a decade when

Cupid's arrow struck in London in 1912. They were at the height of their careers. GBS was haggling over the debut of his most famous play, *Pygmalion*, in the West End. Stella had just come off Broadway, New York, where she'd had yet another glittering success. After years of writing characters based on her (and enduring her rejection of them), GBS finally persuaded her to read for the irresistible lead in *Pygmalion*, Eliza Doolittle. Stella adored the character and agreed to play it. But she then fell seriously ill, and GBS became a fixture at her bedside. He found her gallantry in the face of suffering a transformative experience, and fell much harder and much further in love with Stella than he'd intended.

[Y]ou can only kiss me if I say 'kiss me' and I will never say 'kiss me' because I am a respectable widow and I wouldn't let any man kiss me unless I was sure of the wedding ring ...
Letter from Stella to GBS, 18 Nov 1912

He was fifty-six to Stella's forty-seven, so they were certainly old enough to know what they were doing. She was a widow, still beautiful but about to become a grandmother. He was white-bearded, bushy-browed and married. According to him, his wife, the wealthy Irish suffragette Charlotte Payne-Townshend, was more amused than annoyed about his infatuations. Unfortunately for Charlotte, this infatuation turned out to be more serious.

Their friendship deepened and GBS became obsessed. Gossip in the London literati made its way back to Charlotte, who finally

Stella Tanner, professionally known as Mrs Patrick Campbell.

lost her sense of humour and grew jealous. When Stella made overtures of friendship to Charlotte, she was roundly rejected. Afterwards Charlotte would not even allow her rival's name to be spoken in the house.

When they weren't together, the letters that flowed between GBS and Stella were passionate, savage (GBS), ditsy (Stella), prayerful, comic, and full of hyperbolic endearments, not to mention casual snobbery and racism. There is so much shop talk about plays, venues, actors and money in them that sometimes they are helpfully labelled by their authors either 'Business' or 'Passionate love letter'!

With his usual modesty, GBS often talks of himself in the correspondence as a 'saint and a genius' and often in the third person. He can be brutal: he berates Stella as a cold-hearted temptress, hopes that she loses her beauty so he can prove his sincerity, he calls her unteachable, he warns her against himself, he accuses her of lies and treachery.

As for Stella, she laments that she has been trapped by his talent, his words and his 'Irish character', and that it is too late to do anything but accept and love him the way he is.

The irony is that the love affair was probably celibate – as indeed was GBS's marriage to Charlotte. In their world, it was all about the drama.

The love affair reached a tragi-comic climax in the summer of 1913. Stella went for a week's seaside break to a hotel in Kent, clearly stipulating the need to be alone. But GBS followed her there, hoping for private walks, swims – and possibly a lot more. Faced with the possibility of a ruined reputation and career (not to mention the idea of dealing with GBS full-time), Stella made her feelings clear by disappearing from the hotel with no word of warning and no forwarding address.

GBS was deeply wounded – mainly in his vanity, he later claimed

– and he spent the next year alternately wooing her and rebuking her. 'Promise-breaker,' he wrote, 'cheat, confidence trickster!' Stella scathingly replied, 'You poor thing, unable to understand a mere woman…why should I pay for all your shortcomings?'

Stormy rehearsals for *Pygmalion* continued with Stella and GBS both being difficult. Eventually Stella pulled a diva trick and banned Shaw from the theatre. To his further shock, just before the first night, it emerged that she had secretly married an admirer, George Cornwallis West.

The play was an immense popular success (Stella said the outrageous word 'bloody' onstage, which always brought the house down) and the cast left England to tour with it from July 1914 till 1916. The lovers cooled. In their letters the two now compared themselves to Tristan and Isolde (Iseult), divided by forces beyond their control. They congratulated themselves at having survived their affair intact.

Happy ever after?

GBS and Stella continued to correspond periodically until a year before Stella's death in 1940, though their lives followed different trajectories. Stella lost her son in the war, her husband left her, she had a breakdown and found life as an ageing actress very hard. GBS in the meantime became rich, famous and fêted, and won not only a Nobel Prize for Literature, but also an Oscar for screenwriting on *My Fair Lady*, which was based on *Pygmalion*.

The fickleness of the women I love is equalled only by the
infernal constancy of the women who love me.

Attributed to George Bernard Shaw

Much of their later correspondence was taken up with Stella, now
poverty-stricken, begging her 'brilliant adorable Irish lad' to allow
her to publish their early love letters – after all, hadn't he once said
that everything, even love, should be in the shop window for the
masses to wonder at? Stella claimed they had had a 'gentleman's
agreement', an insurance for the day she ran out of money, and she
even resorted to polite blackmail.

But GBS, unmoved, refused her request.
The further pain and humiliation of
his long-suffering wife was not
something he was prepared to
sanction.

If I have to hurt somebody,
I had better hurt you who are
made of iron and can stand it.

Letter from GBS to Stella,
4 January 1928

For the remainder of Stella's life, GBS would offer advice (some of it even wanted) and also financial help. After both Stella and Charlotte's deaths, he finally sanctioned the publication of both sides of the correspondence, on the condition that the proceeds went to educating Stella's great-grandchildren.

Timeline

26 July 1856 George Bernard Shaw born Portobello, Dublin

9 February 1865 Beatrice Stella Tanner born Kensington, London

1884 Stella elopes with Patrick Campbell and takes his name for the stage

1 June 1898 GBS marries Irish suffragette Charlotte Payne-Townshend

1898 GBS writes title role in his *Cleopatra* for Stella; she declines

6 April 1913 Stella marries Winston Churchill's erstwhile stepfather, George Cornwallis West

August 1913 GBS attempts to rendezvous with Stella in Sandwich, Kent

October 1913 *Pygmalion* first performed, Vienna

1914 *Pygmalion*'s London debut with Stella as Eliza Doolittle

1925 GBS accepts Nobel Prize for Literature but refuses the money

1938 GBS's screenplay of *Pygmalion* earns him an Oscar

9 April 1940 Stella dies, Pau, France

12 September 1943 Charlotte dies, London, England

1946 GBS given the Freedom of Dublin

2 November 1950 GBS dies, London, England

1952 *George Bernard Shaw and Mrs Patrick Campbell: Their Correspondence* published

Opposite: Mrs Patrick Campbell as Eliza Doolittle in *Pygmalion*.

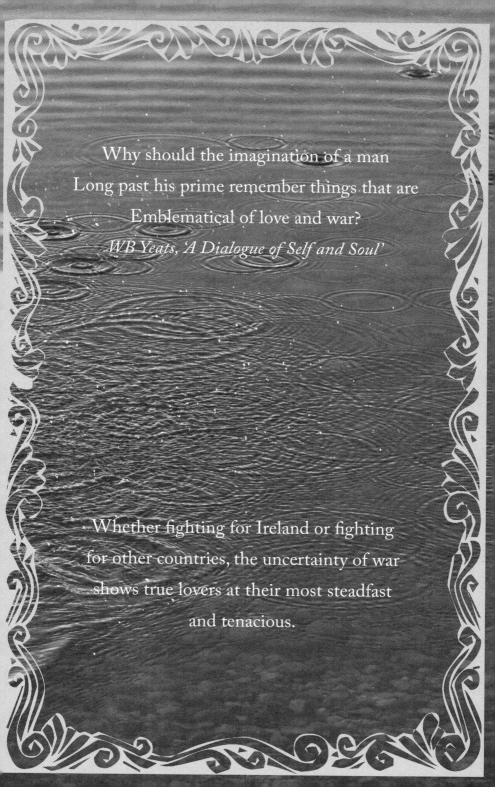

Why should the imagination of a man
Long past his prime remember things that are
Emblematical of love and war?

WB Yeats, 'A Dialogue of Self and Soul'

Whether fighting for Ireland or fighting
for other countries, the uncertainty of war
shows true lovers at their most steadfast
and tenacious.

Kit Kavanagh, also known as Mother Ross, dragoon of the Scots Greys.

Kit Kavanagh & Richard Walsh

I knew no happiness but in possession of Richard Walsh!
Life and Adventures of Mrs Christian Davis (1741)

Cross-dressing pub landlady, Christian 'Kit' Kavanagh, became one of the eighteenth century's most memorable characters because she fooled entire British regiments into thinking she was a male soldier. But the reason she did it all in the first place was for love ...

Kit met Richard Walsh in Dublin in the late 1680s, when she inherited a city tavern from her aunt, and found that the handsome young barman seemed to come with it. According to her 1741 memoir (supposedly taken down by Daniel Defoe), not only was he 'very well made in his person' with 'a handsome, manly face', but he also had an 'open and generous temper' and, astonishingly, was usually sober.

Once Richard realised Kit was interested, he was understandably nervous of the workplace romance. But Kit was a rule bender in sexual politics as in everything else, and what she wanted she tended to get. Today her courtship of Richard reads like a How-Not-To. She encouraged him, then rejected him. She complained he paid her no attention, then accused him of impertinence. One night Richard seized the initiative. He kissed her passionately – then left the room, leaving her to stew. Kit decided they'd better marry quick so they could go to bed, and the next day she proposed. They tied the knot in 1689.

For four years, the loving, hardworking Richard made Kit happy. Business was good, money was coming in, and Kit was pregnant with their third child when it all went dramatically wrong. One night in 1693, Richard went out and never came back.

Out of her mind with shock, Kit sent search parties all over Dublin, but could find out nothing of what had happened to her husband. Eventually she gave up hope and fell into a deep depression.

After the first anniversary of Richard's disappearance had passed, a letter in his handwriting arrived from the Netherlands. It transpired that he had, for the first time in his life, gone on a massive drinking binge, had passed out during a party on his friend's ship and woken up near Antwerp.

I fear I must pass the remainder of a wretched life, under the deepest affliction for my being deprived of the comfort I enjoyed while blessed with you and my dear babies …

Letter from Richard to Kit,
Life and Adventures of Mrs Christian Davis

Richard miserably explained how he couldn't get home because he had no money, and his only means of survival had been to join the army of the English king, William III, then engaged in war with France and Spain. He was stuck, and it was only the thought that he might one day see Kit again that kept him going.

An unheard-of course of action formed in Kit's mind: she was going to find Richard and bring him home. And she was going to do it by joining the army.

Kit left her children with relatives. Then she cut off her hair, flattened her breasts with a bandage, donned Richard's jacket and breeches and enlisted in the infantry as young Christian Walsh. The sergeant accepted her without a second look.

It's hard to imagine what she went through in the first months as a new recruit. She was tall, strong and young, but even so, her physical stamina must have been astonishing. She marched up to twenty miles alongside forty men by day, and bunked down next to them by night. She lowered her voice, concealed her monthly periods and learned to urinate through a tube hidden in her breeches. Luckily, as personal hygiene wasn't a priority in the army, no one took their clothes off to bathe or change.

But Kit never forgot her quest. She asked everyone she met about her 'brother' Richard Walsh. In the meantime, she learned all about army life and found that she loved it. When she transferred regiment to the Scots Greys she fought unscathed at the famous battle of Blenheim. 'The pretty dragoon', as she was nicknamed, certainly had adventures. At one point, she came close to becoming engaged to a young lady. On another occasion, she was named

The Battle of Ramillies by Jan van Huchtenburg, 1706.

in a paternity case, and paid the child maintenance rather than reveal her secret! And it was after this, one day in 1704, following twelve years of summer campaigns over two regiments, that Kit found Richard. She saw him before he saw her – and he was not alone. The blonde woman on his arm was clearly his lover.

Perhaps unreasonably under the circumstances, Kit lost her temper. She had left her home and family, been shot at, wounded, imprisoned, and ransomed, yet here was Richard Walsh of the 1st Foot Guards, large as life and with a Dutch girlfriend, having forgotten all about his wife. In a tavern later that night, she finally ran him to ground.

One can only feel a certain sympathy for the man when Kit's red jacket and tricorn hat came off to reveal a dimly remembered but righteously angry spouse standing in front of him. But once he'd recovered from the shock, Richard swore undying gratitude and love, and promised he would do anything to make amends for his infidelity. Kit announced that the first thing he could do was keep the secret; she had no intention of giving up soldiering. The second thing was they were not to sleep together – a pregnant belly would be tricky to explain to her comrades. Richard agreed to her demands, and for two years that was how they lived.

In 1706, during the Battle of Ramillies, Kit was wounded by a musket ball. It was while she was unconscious that the field surgeon undressed her and discovered her sex. When she awoke it was to a ring of very surprised faces, including that of her brigadier-general Lord John Hay. Kit told her story, which swept around the regiment. Richard corroborated, and Kit became a celebrity overnight.

Lord Hay announced that Kit was 'the best man he'd ever had' in the Scots Greys, and gave her a gift of money. He insisted that she and Richard remarry on the battlefield, which they did with great pomp and ceremony.

Happy ever after?

Kit was allowed to travel with the army – but as a wife only, never again as a soldier. In each summer campaign, her husband went to his work of killing Frenchmen, and she went to hers of looting villages. However, she did get to deploy the sword skills she had learned one more time when she spotted Richard's mistress too close to home. She sliced off the poor woman's nose, before having her ducked in a pond as an adulteress. It did not do to cross a sabre-rattling Mrs Walsh.

My jealousy drove me on too far in this matter.

Life and Adventures of Mrs Christian Davis

After sixteen years in the army, Richard's luck finally ran out at the Battle of Malplaquet. When Kit got the news that he'd been killed she ran to the battlefield and turned over some two hundred bodies before she found him. According to her memoir, intent on vengeance, she had to be dragged away from the French lines by Richard's comrades.

But Kit was a survivor. She would recover, and go on to be married and widowed twice more, both times to soldiers. Commonly called Mother Ross by her comrades because of her friendship with an officer of that name, she lived to a ripe old age in the Royal Chelsea Hospital, London, where she dictated her memoir. She never stopped loving the husband for whom she had changed everything, including her very identity.

Timeline

c. 1665 Richard Walsh born, probably Dublin, Ireland

1667 Kit Kavanagh born, Dublin, Ireland

1689 Kit and Richard marry

c. 1692 Richard disappears, pressed by the Army

1693 Kit enlists as an infantryman

1697 Kit re-enlists as a dragoon in the Scots Greys

1701–14 Kit sees active service in the War of the Spanish Succession

11 September 1709 Richard killed in action, Battle of Malplaquet, France

1712 Kit presented to Queen Anne and receives a pension

7 July 1739 Kit dies, Chelsea Royal Hospital, London, England

1741 *The Life and Adventures of Mrs Christian Davis* published, formerly attributed to Daniel Defoe

'Eva' of *The Nation*, *c.* 1860s.

'—Eva' Kelly &
Kevin O'Doherty

O sweet wind, speed across the wave/As fast as fast may be;
There's someone there that would be glad/To hear some news of me.
'Eva' of *The Nation*, 'To the Wandering Wind' (1909)

In the summer of 1848, against the grim backdrop of starvation and revolt in Ireland, a popular poet and a political prisoner met, fell in love – and were immediately forced apart with the whole, wide world between them.

Mary Anne Kelly, or 'Eva' as she was professionally known, was a precocious fifteen-year-old when she sent poems to the new nationalist weekly, *The Nation*. Within three years, she had become one of the very few youthful female voices in Ireland's independence struggle.

One admirer of her poems was twenty-four-year-old Kevin Izod O'Doherty, an energetic six-footer with ruddy cheeks, high forehead and wonderfully bushy whiskers. By day, Kevin studied medicine; but by night, he fomented rebellion as part of the Young Ireland movement. He was also the co-editor of the inflammatory *Irish Tribune*, which printed ideas such as fair pay for workers and American-style insurrection against the Crown. It was the latter that landed him and his comrades in prison under the Treason Felony Act, which had recently been passed by Parliament – particularly with the rebellious Young Irelanders in mind.

Eva and Kevin met for the first time in a prison cell when she, along with other lady supporters of the Young Ireland movement, visited Dublin's Newgate. With dark, dreamy eyes and black, wavy hair cascading down to her knees, Eva looked every inch the romantic heroine. The chemistry was palpable and soon Eva had dispensed with her chaperones and was coming to see Kevin on her own. The romance and tragedy of their situation made rational thought all but impossible. They fell in love with each other – and they were in love with Ireland.

Back in the real world, Kevin went to trial not once but twice with inconclusive verdicts. This was due to widespread sympathy among the jury. (In Clonmel, several Young Irelanders had been sentenced to hanging.) Concerned by the bad publicity, the authorities asked Kevin if he would agree a compromise: If he would *privately* plead guilty, they would let him go.

It was a tempting offer. Kevin had his whole life ahead of him. He wanted to marry Eva Kelly, and qualify as a doctor. But Eva's reaction was unyielding: she told Kevin that she would wait any length of time for him rather than see him agree to such a dishonourable bargain with the enemy.

We can only imagine what Kevin's feelings were when he heard this – one hopes they perfectly coincided with his fiancée's. He agreed to fight on but when his third trial came around in October

Kevin O'Doherty, *c.* 1860s.

1848, Dublin Castle packed the jury with enough Crown supporters to convict him. Eva watched in horror as he got the maximum
sentence of ten years penal servitude in Van Diemen's Land (Tasmania). 'I'll wait,' she whispered as he was taken away in chains,
aware that she might be saying goodbye not just to Kevin but also
her chance of a home, marriage and children.

It took four months for Kevin's ship to reach Tasmania, the most
feared convict settlement in Australia. Kevin and the other Irish
rebels were luckier than many – they were categorised as ticket-of-
leave men instead of common criminals, which meant they could
live in the community under probation. It was now that Kevin
acquired the nickname Saint Kevin, given to him by John Mitchel
in his *Jail Journal*, for the religious young man bore the separation
from his beloved Eva as a penance. Several of Kevin's comrades,
including Mitchel, escaped to America, but Kevin chose instead
to stay and use his training to work as an assistant surgeon in a
Hobart hospital – another reason, perhaps, for his holy nickname.

Meanwhile, back in Ireland, Eva carried on composing poetry.
She became more radical in Kevin's absence, pouring her anguish
into her work, such as the stirring 'Down, Britannia, Down!'. For
example, in 'The Patriot Mother' one woman is uncompromising in her view on informers, even if they turn out to be her own
children:

Alanna, Alanna! the shadow of shame
Has never yet fall'n upon one of your name,

And, oh, may the food from my bosom you drew,

In your veins turn to poison, if you turn untrue.

Her poetry made her a celebrity, stirred sympathy and provided funding for the Irish Cause.

Kevin served six years in Tasmania. In 1854 he was released on a conditional pardon, the condition being that he stay away from Ireland. Of course, no man with a beauty waiting for him was going to pay attention to this stricture. The lovers' meeting in Galway was ecstatic. A timely inheritance was handed over to Kevin, so the couple could finally make plans to marry. When word got out to the police that 'a strange gentleman' was in Galway, the plans had to be accelerated, and Kevin and Eva hot-footed it to England. A small, quiet wedding took place in London, and the pair left for Paris soon after.

As soon as Kevin's full pardon came through in 1856, they returned to Dublin, where Eva had the first of her eight children. After a ten-year delay, Kevin was finally able to qualify as a doctor. All was set fair – but the O'Dohertys were never the type to settle for cosy domesticity.

Happy ever after?

In 1860 the family headed back to Australia and settled in Queensland. Kevin became a leading light in state politics and religious affairs, as well as running a successful medical practice and campaigning for public health measures. Eva's radicalism waned with each new baby, the rushing torrent of her poetic output decreased until it was a slow, decidedly non-revolutionary trickle.

Then in 1885, nearly forty years after the adventures of rebellious youth landed him in prison, Kevin entered the political fray once again. Back in London, the Irish Parliamentary Party's battle for Home Rule was tantalisingly close to being won under the leadership of Charles Stewart Parnell. Kevin crossed the globe to be elected MP for North Meath. But his life as a parliamentarian did not last long for the simple reason that, after the Home Rule Bill was defeated in 1886 and another general election was called, he did not have the funds to fight it.

Kevin returned to Australia once more, where sadly the uncertainties of his and Eva's youth were reprised in their old age – but with far less happy outcomes. Seven of their eight children predeceased them in more or less tragic circumstances. Kevin went blind. They became very poor, eventually selling their home and most of their possessions. After his death, Eva relied on support from her surviving daughter, and from the Irish-Australian community.

The feisty Eva published her last volume of poetry in 1909, a year before her own death. She and Kevin O'Doherty are buried next to each other under a Celtic cross in Toowong near Brisbane in Queensland.

Timeline

7 September 1823 Kevin Izod O'Doherty born in Gloucester St, Dublin, Ireland

15 February *c.* 1830 Mary Anne 'Eva' Kelly born near Headford, County Galway, Ireland

1842 *The Nation* newspaper established in Dublin as part of Daniel O'Connell's Repeal
movement

1845 Eva's first poem, 'The Leprechaun', appears in *The Nation*

1848 Kevin imprisoned for sedition

1849 Kevin convicted and transported to Van Diemen's Land (Tasmania)

1845–53 Eva continues to write for *The Nation*

March 1855 Kevin, released on condition he avoids Ireland, travels illegally to Galway

23 August 1855 Eva and Kevin marry

1857 Kevin becomes a Fellow of the Royal College of Surgeons (FRCS)

1867 Kevin becomes a politician in Queensland, Australia

1877 Eva publishes a collection of 180 poems in USA

1885 Kevin elected Irish Parliamentary Party MP to House of Commons, England

15 July 1905 Kevin dies in Brisbane, Queensland, Australia

1909 *Poems by 'Eva' of The Nation* published

22 May 1910 Eva dies in Brisbane, Queensland, Australia

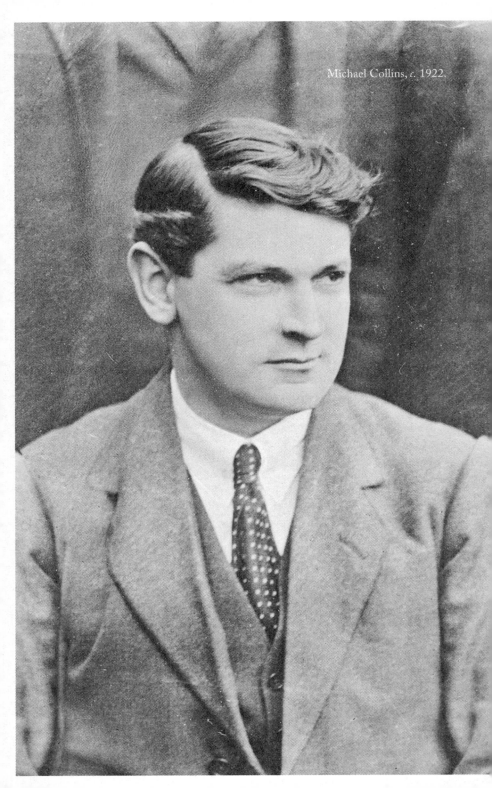
Michael Collins, *c*. 1922.

Michael Collins & Kitty Kiernan

What has happened to you ... not to have written for three days[?]

Letter from Michael to Kitty (1922)

In 1918, World War I was not yet over, and Ireland's War of Independence had not yet begun, but pretty 'Kitty' Kiernan from Granard, County Longford, was not interested in a ravaged Europe nor in the growing turbulence in her own country. Instead, according to the Glasnevin Trust, this vivacious twenty-six-year-old loved novels, dancing, late mornings, fine clothes and romance.

Kitty's lively personality and lovely looks attracted not one but two senior Irish Republican Brotherhood (IRB) men – Michael Collins and his friend and comrade Harry Boland. All three met when Michael and Harry were canvassing the local area on behalf of Sinn Féin, and stepped into the Greville Arms, where Kitty lived and worked with her four siblings. There seems to have been a degree of flirtation and fluidity in all their relationships; Harry was attracted to Kitty, while Michael, 'the Big Fella', as he was known, was initially more interested in one of her sisters. But when that sister became engaged, Michael switched his focus to Kitty, apparently unfazed by his friend's attachment.

For months Michael and Harry engaged in an open rivalry for Kitty's affections. The girl must have felt spoilt for choice with the tough, courageous Harry on the one hand and the brilliant, charismatic Michael on the other, both vying for her attention, all against the backdrop of rebellion against the British.

But Fate was about to step in in the shape of 'the Chief', Eamon de Valera. During the War of Independence in 1919–21, he sent Harry off on trips to the USA to raise funds (and perhaps buy a few guns while he was there), while Michael went on the run. Back in Granard, love letters arrived for Kitty, either from America (Harry), or from a variety of barns, safe houses and hideaways (Michael).

By the time a truce was called between the Irish and the British in July 1921, Kitty's situation was still a triangle. But when Harry had to return to the USA yet again, Michael took the opportunity to push home his advantage, constantly writing and visiting whenever he could. From October until Christmas 1921, Michael was to-ing and fro-ing to London, part of the delegation negotiating the all-important Anglo-Irish Treaty. Here Michael's life hit new heights of feverish activity. Tricky negotiations with the Prime Minister took place during the day – but unofficial, social meetings at the home of the beautiful Lady Hazel Lavery and her Irish painter husband John oiled the political wheels every evening. Lady Hazel not only drove Michael around London when he needed but also met him at Mass every morning, so it wasn't long before rumours were swirling across the Irish Sea to Kitty's ears. Though Lady Hazel, whose face adorned the Irish pound note for more than fifty years,

Kitty Kiernan outside the Greville Arms Hotel, Granard, County Longford.

subsequently admitted she had been smitten by the looks and personality of Michael Collins, there is no evidence that Michael was ever unfaithful to his dearest Kitty.

Be all that as it may, Michael proposed to Kitty, who accepted. They planned to marry in the autumn of 1922 in a double wedding with Kitty's sister, Maud, and her fiancé, IRB officer Gearóid O'Sullivan. Harry Boland accepted his defeat with grace. He wrote to Kitty: 'I want to congratulate you. M [Mick] told me of your engagement, and I wish you long life and happiness.'

Happy ever after?

In early 1922, the Dáil passed the Treaty partitioning away six counties of Ireland by just seven votes, and civil war erupted in Ireland. As is always the case with civil war, former comrades now found they were on opposite sides and, in the case of Michael and Harry, love rivals became rivals in war. Michael was commander-in-chief of the pro-Treaty Free State Army, whose aim was to crush the opposition of the anti-Treaty Irregulars that included Harry Boland.

It was a dangerous world to live in. On 31 July 1922, Harry was shot and fatally wounded by a Free State soldier, whose name he refused to reveal, even on his deathbed. After attending Harry's funeral, Kitty pressed the ever more distraught Michael to marry her, so she could be with him and look after him as his wife. Tragically, before a day could be named, Michael too was shot dead in an ambush at Béal na mBláth in his home county of Cork.

It is said that Kitty had a breakdown after losing Michael. Just two months after his death, on the wedding day that should have been her own, she watched as Maud married Gearóid. She wore black from head to toe.

Kitty slowly got her life back together. She married a comrade of Michael's and had two children, one of whom was named after her dead love. Before she died of kidney disease, aged just fifty-two, Kitty asked to be buried near Michael in Glasnevin Cemetery, and this wish was granted.

Timeline

27 April 1887 Harry Boland born Phibsborough, Dublin

16 October 1890 Michael Collins born Woodfield, County Cork

26 January 1893 Catherine Brigid ('Kitty') Kiernan born Granard, County Longford

1908 Kiernan parents die, leaving sixteen-year-old Kitty and siblings to run the Greville Arms Hotel, Granard

1917 Kitty meets Harry

1918 Kitty meets Michael

1919–1921 War of Independence

July 1921 Anglo-Irish Truce

6 December 1921 Anglo-Irish Treaty signed

1922–23 Irish Civil War

1 August 1922 Harry dies of wounds received in an ambush by Free State Army

22 August 1922 Michael killed by Irregulars

10 June 1925 Kitty marries army officer Felix Cronin, and has two sons

24 July 1945 Kitty dies, Dublin

10th April 1922

My dearest Kitty

No letter again today as I got back from Wexford late last night but it was only this morning I got your wire. There was a very good meeting at Wexford and a very good reception all along both going and coming. No interruption at all at the meeting.

What has happened to you though seriously not to have written for three days I suppose you've been enjoying yourself too well or something — staying up at night and in bed at day. Is that it? How did the hunt go on? Honestly I do think it a shame

2

you haven't written — but then I may be hard on you there may be a real reason and if I said anything — but then I don't say anythings that I have to regret afterwards.

Things are rapidly becoming as bad as they can be and the country has before it what may be the worst period yet. A few madmen may do anything. Indeed they are just getting on the pressure gradually — they go on from cutting a tree to cutting a railway line, then tofiring at a barrack, then to firing at a lorry, and so on. But God knows I do not want

3

to be worrying you with these
things.
Are you going to Nobbe for
Easter? Or are you going anywhere
I'm most awfully anxious to see
you quickly and this week is
going to be a bad week with
me by the look of things. Any
improvement in the Connemara
plans yet? Kitty do please
hurry with making that definite
but I am anxious about you.
I wonder if you're writing even
to-day — yes? No?
May God bless you
Fondest love Miceal

Michael and Kitty wrote to each other nearly every day.

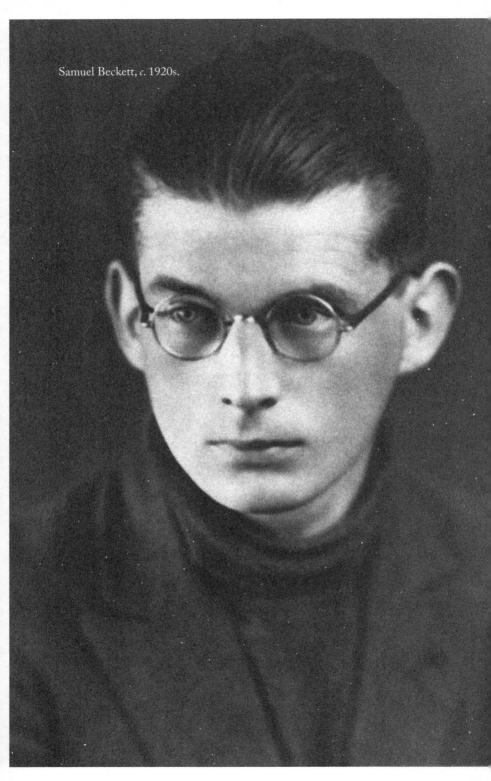
Samuel Beckett, *c.* 1920s.

Samuel Beckett & Suzanne Déchevaux-Dumesnil

if you do not love me I shall not be loved

if I do not love you I shall not love …

Samuel Beckett, *Cascando and Other Short Dramatic Pieces*

Romantic, in a bleak way. And very Samuel Beckett, the man who felt that in love – as in life – we are all lonely failures. Not that it stopped him from trying …

Sam, as friends called him, met Suzanne Déchevaux-Dumesnil when both were members of Paris's arty, writerly avant-garde set, living the Bohemian dream in the 1930s. He was a writer, a six-foot, blue-eyed, big-eared Dubliner, with a serious expression etched onto his craggy face. She was a pianist, a chic, dark-eyed, cleft-chinned Frenchwoman, with modern bobbed hair and fashionable clothes.

They were already slight acquaintances, having played at a tennis party, but on 6 January 1938 an event took place that drew them together in dramatic circumstances.

Sam had spent that wintry evening with two friends, and was making his way home off the Avenue d'Orleans when a pimp approached and started to harass him. The pimp wanted Sam's money or his custom, and finally became so incensed at getting nowhere that he took out a knife and plunged it into Beckett's ribs, just missing his heart and lung.

Sam slumped to the ground, bleeding massively. His two friends carried him back to their apartment, where they called an ambulance.

In the Hôpital Broussais, where James Joyce insisted on paying for a private room, Sam floated near death for a week. Shocked family from Ireland and Parisian friends gathered around him, including Suzanne. He suffered damage to the lining of the lung in the attack, and bore the scars for the rest of his life, but he was young and strong. He recovered enough to become interested in his attractive visitor, and soon a relationship was blossoming.

But there was a complication. For the previous year, Sam had been having a lot of no-strings sex with the fiery heiress and art collector, Peggy Guggenheim, who had fallen hard for him. Sam now had to disentangle himself from one affair, pursue another, recuperate from a near-fatal stabbing and deal with continual rejections from publishers all at the same time.

I would like my love to die/and the rain to be falling on the graveyard

and on me walking the streets/mourning her who thought
she loved me.

Samuel Beckett, *Poems in English and French* (1963)

Luckily for Sam, in this triangle, Suzanne was calm and independent, where Peggy was dramatic and needy. At thirty-eight,
Suzanne was six years older than Sam, with, according to James
Knowlson, Sam's official biographer, a mature and generous out-
look. Like Sam, she was outdoorsy, private and loyal. 'Tiny and
tenacious' was how the playwright Fernando Arrabal described her.

Sam continued to see Peggy on and off over the first six months
of his new relationship (not least because she helped him in his
career). But when he started making excuses not to spend the
night, Peggy knew that Suzanne was winning the battle for Sam's
heart. She conceded as gracefully as she could: 'She made curtains,
while I made scenes,' she said of her rival.

It was not the first time Sam had had to navigate a tricky
love life. Ten years earlier, he had been part of the literary circle
of James Joyce, and assisted with what would become *Finnegans
Wake*. During this work, Joyce's daughter Lucia had developed a
deep crush on Sam. His attempts to distance himself from Lucia
preceded a breakdown in the girl (who went on to develop schizo-
phrenia). Joyce, feeling outrage in the paternal breast at what he
perceived as a young buck trifling with his adored daughter, ousted
Sam from the circle.

The 1930s came to an explosive end with the outbreak of World

The village of Roussillon, Provence-Alpes-Côte d'Azur, southwest France, where Résistance members Sam and Suzanne hid from the Nazis from 1942 to 1945.

War II. Sam was in Ireland at the time but, refusing to abandon either Suzanne or their Jewish friends, he rushed back to Paris. 'I prefer France at war to Ireland at peace,' he said.

Ireland's neutrality would have protected him, if Sam had chosen to live quietly and remain safe. But he and Suzanne were not made that way. In 1941 when the Gestapo started to arrest their friends, they chose to become active members of the Résistance. Suzanne was, as usual, competent in everything she touched, whether it was a sewing machine or a firearm, but Sam, despite having been a terrific cricketer back in Ireland, turned out to be a terrible shot. He switched to secretly translating, summarising and passing on crucial information to contacts in Paris.

In 1942 their cell was betrayed. Sam and Suzanne received a tip-off from the wife of one of their arrested friends that they had just a couple of hours before the Gestapo came to their apartment. They grabbed a few essentials and fled Paris.

After six weeks travelling by night and hiding in barns, parks and in friends' houses, they made it to a rented house in the red hills of Roussillon in Provence, which became their home for the next three years. (Today the village holds an annual Beckett festival.)

Here Sam and Suzanne had to work the land to get barely enough food to survive. They lived as anonymously as possible, and when German soldiers came through, they hid in a cave concealed behind a pile of logs.

Again they aided the Résistance – this time by storing ammunition in their home and outbuildings. According to Knowlson, this indirectly helped sabotage the German army in the Vaucluse mountains.

It wasn't all bad. Sam and Suzanne's flight, their trust in and reliance on each other released a surge of creativity in the writer. It was in Roussillon that Sam wrote most of his novel, *Watt*, and conceived the idea for his most famous play *Waiting for Godot* (1949). The village is referenced in the second act.

Sam rarely spoke about his war, but he suffered from depression afterwards. It was Suzanne who dragged him through the black days and drinking binges that later dogged him, and got him writing again. It was she who protected and promoted his work and negotiated with agents and publishers on his behalf.

Happy ever after?

The couple reached an unconventional accommodation about monogamy. Sam was not a womaniser but he was not exclusive either. He categorized sex separately from love or friendship, and he considered Suzanne to be separate from everyone else. Suzanne, with her own group of close friends to rely on, seems to have allowed him this freedom. In their Paris home in Boulevard St Jacques they used separate bedrooms and entrances, while Beckett used his country home for rendezvous.

When he was in his fifties, Sam met the second great love of his life, the BBC literary translator Barbara Bray, a widow in her thirties with two children. Despite the age gap, she fell in love with the generous and enigmatic genius almost immediately, especially, as she later recalled, with his voice, which she described as sounding like the sea. The ensuing affair was cerebral, as well as physical, with Sam finding, once again, a highly intelligent, cultured woman with whom he could discuss his work. Barbara would act as Sam's confidante and champion for the rest of his life. (Today Trinity College Dublin holds more than 700 letters from the author to Barbara.)

After four years, Barbara moved to Paris to be close to Sam. And his response? He immediately organised a wedding – for himself and Suzanne. It's likely that he wanted to ensure Suzanne's future security by ensuring she retained the rights over his estate. The triangular relationship lasted for the rest of his life and informed, some academics claim, his 1963 work, *Play*.

In the event, Suzanne didn't need the security of marriage. She died before Sam on 17 July 1989, and he followed five months later on 22 December. The two share a simple granite gravestone in Montparnasse Cemetery in Paris, which had to be, by Sam's stipulation, 'any colour, so long as it's grey'.

Timeline

7 January 1900 Suzanne Déchevaux-Dumesnil born in Troyes, France

13 April 1906 Samuel Barclay Beckett born in Foxrock, County Dublin, Ireland

24 November 1924 Barbara Jacobs (later Bray) born Maida Vale, London, England

1928, Sam moves to Paris after graduating from Trinity College Dublin (with both a gold medal and a scholarship)

1941 Sam and Suzanne join the French Résistance

August 1942, Sam and Suzanne flee south to the small village of Roussillon, in the Vaucluse département in Provence-Alpes-Côte d'Azur

1945 Sam is awarded the Croix de Guerre and the Médaille de la Résistance by the French government for what he called his 'boy scout stuff'

1947–50 Beckett writes *Molloy, Malone Dies, Waiting for Godot, The Unnameable* – all in French

1953 Sam builds a country retreat on land near Ussy-sur-Marne around sixty kilometres (forty miles) northeast of Paris

1957 Sam meets Barbara while working on his play *All That Fall* for BBC radio

1961 Sam and Suzanne marry in a Folkestone registry office; Barbara moves to Paris

1969 Sam wins Nobel Prize for Literature, which Suzanne, concerned that the burden of fame would upset their reclusive, intensely private lifestyle, describes as *'une catastrophe'*

17 July 1989 Suzanne dies, Paris, France

22 December 1989 Sam dies, Paris, France

25 February 2010 Barbara dies, Edinburgh, Scotland

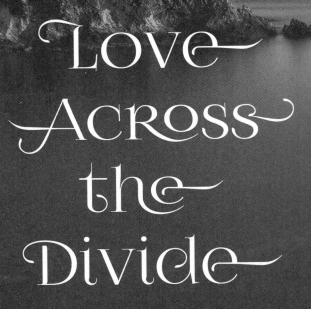

Love Across the Divide

You were the moonlight, I lived in the sun;
Could there ever be peace between us twain?

Eva Gore-Booth, 'The Body to the Soul'

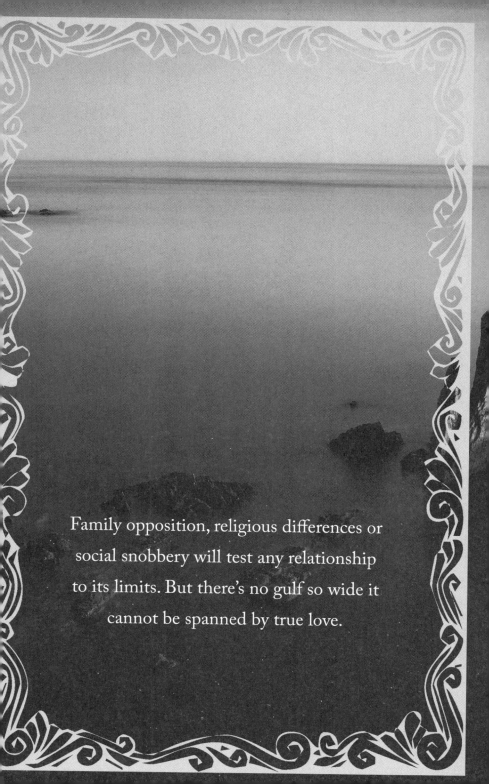

Family opposition, religious differences or
social snobbery will test any relationship
to its limits. But there's no gulf so wide it
cannot be spanned by true love.

Just married – Mr and Mrs Sean O'Casey outside the Church of Our Most Holy Redeemer and St Thomas More, Chelsea, 1927.

Sean O'Casey & Eileen Carey

It was a joy to be with him and to listen.

Eileen O'Casey, *Sean* (1971)

There is nothing more unwavering than a young actress in search of a good role. But when beautiful Eileen Carey journeyed across the Atlantic to meet the dramatist Sean O'Casey, she landed not just a part in his play, but also the central role in his life.

In 1926 Eileen was twenty-five years old and working in the chorus of a Broadway hit. Born in Dublin but brought up in English boarding schools, she was homeless and alone in the world, apart from her estranged mother in London. Eileen loved the theatre but was exhausted by doing eight shows a week, modelling on the side and avoiding New York's infamous casting couches. When a copy of the new tragi-comedy *Juno and the Paycock* by Sean O'Casey fell into her lap, she devoured it in one sitting. Its raw emotion left her reeling; she felt strongly drawn to the writer, and she wanted a part in one of his plays. But she was in New York and Sean O'Casey was in London. How could she get to him?

In London's aptly named Fortune Theatre, the author of *Juno* was experiencing a seismic lucky streak. At forty-six, Sean O'Casey was an awkward character, stubborn, self-educated and disillusioned with the new Irish Free State's failure to live up to his passionate socialist ideals. He had spent most of his adult life in impoverished obscurity, writing plays and poems in his mother's tenement until she died when he was thirty-eight. Since then, he'd been living hand to mouth in bedsits while his plays caused minor riots in Dublin's Abbey Theatre. He had never had any luck in love. Until now.

Just days after disembarking at Southampton, Eileen persuaded her married lover, theatre manager Lee Ephraim, to arrange a meeting with Sean at the Fortune. When she walked in, heads turned for, as Sean later wrote, with her laughing face and fantastic figure, she was the loveliest lass he had ever seen in his life. As for Eileen, she was impressed in a different way by the gaunt figure with the penetrating hazel eyes. It wasn't love at first sight, but it was excitement; his voice and the power of his words fascinated her. Again luck played its part: an actress in the London production of Sean's *The Plough and the Stars* fell ill, and he immediately chose Eileen for the role of Nora.

It was a big challenge for an inexperienced young woman but Sean was encouraging. With his support, Eileen pulled it off and the play was a critical success. Then the original actress recovered, and Eileen was unceremoniously let go.

A chance meeting in Bond Street changed the relationship from professional to personal. In debt, unwell and overworked, Eileen found she could confide in Sean, who was a brilliant talker but an even better listener. In a teashop, they discussed losing their fathers too young, Sean's fight for the workers of Dublin, Eileen's breakdown and her fear of the mental illness that dogged her family. A gentle courtship ensued.

Sean and Eileen had much more in common than sceptical onlookers supposed. Eileen had insight: she knew she needed a father-figure as a companion, so the twenty-year age gap between her and Sean was an attraction, not an obstacle. Both had been bereaved and uprooted as children, and Sean needed a protector and homemaker so that he could work. Both were in love with the theatre and neither, as Eileen admitted, had 'any damned sense of money at all'.

There were differences too. Unlike Sean, Eileen hadn't a political bone in her body, but she did have the people skills that Sean lacked. His writing had made him powerful enemies in Ireland, including the Catholic hierarchy, the Gaelic League, Sinn Féin and WB Yeats. Eileen, in contrast, made and kept friends wherever she went. She was gregarious, while Sean was introverted and reclusive. It could have been a recipe for disaster, but he encouraged her to live her life fully, so long as she took care of her health.

In her wonderful 1971 autobiography *Sean*, Eileen describes how her unmaterialistic suitor bought no gifts of jewels or furs. Instead, he presented her with macaroons, and paid off her debts with what money he had. Meanwhile, Eileen struggled to choose between Sean (single but poor) and Lee (well-off but married). Her mother didn't help. She opposed the idea of marriage to Sean on the grounds of religion, age difference and financial prospects, and told Sean he was ruining her daughter's life. (However, Eileen's mother was to allow him to support her financially for the rest of hers.)

In the end, resolution came from an unexpected quarter. When

Sean bumped into Lee on Eileen's doorstep, he braced himself to fight the younger, bigger man and the two disappeared around the corner. Whether fisticuffs ensued or not, Sean returned alone with a concrete proposal, which Eileen accepted. It was timely; she was already two months pregnant with his baby.

Since Eileen was a Catholic, albeit somewhat lukewarm, Sean suffered being married in a church side chapel, where mixed unions between Protestants and Catholics took place. As an atheist, he couldn't take any religious ceremony seriously, which was just as well, for the day was full of comic incident. Sean appeared with a large burn in the seat of his trousers, Eileen's mother wore black and tried to prevent the priest from entering his church, the best man mislaid the ring, and Eileen's heartbroken ex turned up and wept throughout the wedding. All was captured by the reporters crowding in, and a news camera rolling.

The two fell in love deeply during their six-week honeymoon in Howth, County Dublin, and would stay married, through financial hardship, controversy and bereavement for the next thirty-seven years.

Happy ever after?

In every home they lived in, Eileen recreated for Sean his writing room, a den with a single bed and a coal fire, which resembled the bedsits he'd occupied in Dublin. He worked wearing a series of colourful hats (one of which he donated to Samuel Beckett to use in his play, *Happy Days*). Passionate about her husband's writing and always putting him and their three children first, she also managed to meet her own social and sexual needs outside the marriage, most notably with Harold Macmillan, the future prime minister. Sean was a highly unusual man for that, or indeed any, time; the years the O'Caseys spent together were unencumbered with jealousy, and filled with acceptance.

> You are and have been indeed, *Cuisle mo craidhe* [sic], the pulse of my heart; and this heart of mine loves you, and will unto the last. Oh, my darling girl.
>
> Sean's dying message to Eileen, *Sean*

The second half of Sean O'Casey's life was characterised by international acclaim, and a continued contrariness (he refused every accolade and honour). He was at the pinnacle of his fame when, tragically, he and Eileen lost their beloved middle child to leukaemia. Eileen subsequently attempted suicide, but somehow, through work, they got through their grief. Eileen read to him every day when Sean went blind and she remained what he called 'the stalwart of the O'Casey home'.

After Sean's death at the age of eighty-four, Eileen made the most of a long and sprightly widowhood, writing well-received memoirs, lecturing on life with O'Casey and maintaining close links with theatre people, including Samuel Beckett. She ended her days, still a beautiful woman, in a home for retired actors.

Timeline

30 March 1880 Sean O'Casey born John Casey, 85 Upper Dorset Street, Dublin

27 December 1900 Eileen Reynolds, later known as Carey, born in Dublin, reared in London

c. 1894 Sean starts work, aged fourteen, as a labourer

1914 Sean meets James Larkin; helps draw up the constitution of James Connolly's Irish Citizen Army

1916 Eileen suffers a breakdown

1923 O'Casey's first accepted play, *The Shadow of a Gunman*, debuts at the Abbey Theatre, Dublin; Eileen debuts in the chorus line for the D'Oyly Carte Company, taking her mother's maiden name

1924 *Juno and the Paycock* debuts at the Abbey

1925 Eileen sings and dances in *Rose Marie*

1926 *The Plough and the Stars* debuts at the Abbey to booing from Sinn Féin members of the audience

1927 Eileen appears in *The Plough and the Stars* and The Shadow of a Gunman in London productions

23 September 1927 Sean and Eileen marry

1928 Sean publishes Yeats's rejection of *The Silver Tassie* in *The Irish Times*, starting a public row; his *Within the Gates* is banned in Boston

1928 Breon born; 1935 Niall born; 1939 Shivaun born

1938 Eileen and Sean relocate to Devon, first Totnes, then Torquay

1957 Eileen and Sean lose Niall to leukaemia; Eileen subsequently attempts suicide

1958 Archbishop of Dublin demands withdrawal of Sean's play *The Drums of Father Ned* from Dublin's Tostál festival; Samuel Beckett responds by withdrawing his own work

18 September 1964 Sean dies in Torquay and is cremated at the Golders Green Crematorium

9 April 1995 Eileen dies in London and her ashes scattered in the same place as Sean's

Estella Solomons & Seumas O'Sullivan

Free through the world your spirit goes,
Forbidden hands are clasping yours.

Eva Gore-Booth, 'Comrades' (*c.* 1916*)*

The love affair of Estella and Seumas, or Jimmy as he was sometimes known, was a slow, steady burner. But despite taking place over nearly twenty years against insurmountable family objection, not to mention national revolution, its flame never went out.

The artist Estella Solomons met the poet James Sullivan Starkey (pen name Seumas O'Sullivan) in Dublin in the first decade of the twentieth century, probably around 1909, when they were both in their twenties. Estella's portraits of Seumas from the period show he was good-looking, with a high forehead and gentle face, largely obscured by a fashionable moustache. He was famous for his dry wit. Her own self-portraits show large, soulful eyes, an enviable shock of dark hair and a serious expression, the latter evidence of her steely backbone. In personality, they were modest and quiet-natured, with Seumas occasionally breaking out of chronic shyness with the help of alcohol, and Estella using a ladylike demeanour to mask her rebellious character.

Their artistic temperaments made them a perfect match, but there was a problem – Estella's parents were Jewish, her father from one of Ireland's oldest and most distinguished families. (Both he and her brother, a top doctor and international rugby player, get a mention in Joyce's novels *Ulysses* and *Finnegans Wake*.) Seumas, whose grandfather had been a prominent Methodist preacher and who was

himself a Christian, was a highly unsuitable husband.

The Irish Jewish community was small, peaking at less than five thousand in the early part of the twentieth century. One way to keep Jewish faith and culture alive, argued the elders, was to strongly discourage young people from marrying outside the faith. Estella was told that she would be excluded from her father's will if she married Seumas but still she refused to give him up. Caught

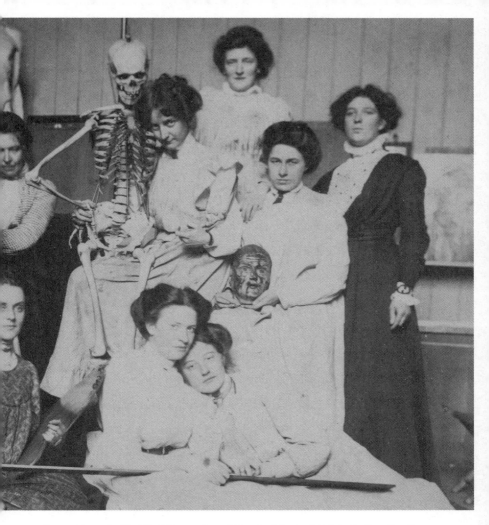

Artists from the Dublin Metropolitan School of Art, *c.* 1910, including Estella Solomons (seated on right, holding a head).

between causing her parents irreparable pain and losing the love of her life, what could she do? Answer: she developed a zen-like patience and implacability. Instead of a showdown, a subtle accommodation was reached. Estella continued to live at home in Waterloo Road, but rented a studio at 17 Great Brunswick Street (now Pearse Street), which gave her a measure of independence.

Here, she spent much time with Seumas, who described it as 'a place of refuge'. She postponed indefinitely any plan to marry.

Along with personal turmoil, there were other major distractions in those restless times. Seumas's Unionist family had always urged him not to 'go Irish', but he and Estella were active Republicans. He published *Requiem and Other Poems* in 1917, which elegised the Easter Rising leaders, while Estella joined Cumann na mBan (the women-only auxiliary of the nationalist Irish Volunteers), and hid ammunition for the Volunteers in her family's vegetable patch. She also stole the uniform of her visiting brother-in-law, a British Army officer, and passed it on to the Volunteers.

During the War of Independence and subsequent Civil War, Estella used her studio to hide IRA men 'on the run', either from the British authorities or the Irish Free State, and painted many of them, including Frank Aiken, Frank Gallagher, Erskine Childers and Sean Milroy. How it must have hurt when she had to burn her own work during the all-too-frequent raids, lest the portraits help the Free State Government track down her friends.

Happy ever after?

In 1926, after the death of Estella's father, the couple were finally able to marry and move into a house in Rathgar.

Together the artist and the poet became important figures in Dublin's cultural life. From 1923, a serious literary venture, *The Dublin Magazine*, became central to their life, especially Seumas's, who did most of the editorial work, supported by Estella's fund-raising and artistry. The magazine became a renowned quarterly, featuring fiction, poetry, drama and reviews from every significant Irish writer; Seamus gave the playwright Samuel Beckett and the poet Patrick Kavanagh their start when no other publication would touch them. The O'Solomons, as Dublin wits called them, hosted legendary at-homes for literary figures and, according to academic Dr Róisín Kennedy, maintained a library containing ten thousand books.

Timeline

17 July 1879 James Sullivan Starkey born 7 Charleston Avenue, Dublin, Ireland

2 April 1882 Esther 'Estella' Frances Solomons born 32 Waterloo Road, Dublin, Ireland

1898 Estella studies at Dublin's Metropolitan School of Art

1902 James publishes first poem in *The Homestead*

1903–06 Estella studies at London's Chelsea School of Art

1903 James adopts pseudonym Seumas O'Sullivan (at writer Padraic Colum's suggestion)

1905 Seumas publishes his first collection, *The Twilight People*

1910 Estella takes on a studio at 17 Great Brunswick Street

c. 1918 Estella joins the Rathmines branch of Cumann na mBan

1923 Estella forced to resign from her school for refusing to take the Oath of Allegiance to the Crown; Seumas starts new literary magazine

5 August 1926 Estella and Seumas marry at Seumas's brother's house in Wales

1939 Seumas awarded honorary doctorate from UCD

24 March 1958 Seumas dies, Dublin, Ireland

1966 Estella finally made honorary member of the Royal Hibernian Academy after showing annually as an associate member more than forty years

2 November 1968 Estella dies, Dublin, Ireland

Winifred Carney.

Winifred Carney & George McBride

She was republican. He was unionist ... She had fought against England. He had fought for England. She was too old for him. He was too young for her ...

Allison Murphy, *Winnie and George: An Unlikely Union* (2016)

The love story of Winnie and George is touching, romantic and unexpected, crossing a cultural chasm and an age divide, flouting religious and social convention but resulting in a famously happy union.

It was 1924 in Belfast, Northern Ireland, and although it may have been the roaring twenties in some quarters, there were sadly few flappers, jazz clubs and cocktail parties in the newly fledged statelet. Belfast was infamous for its poor wages and lack of rights, and it was a shared sense of the sickening injustice visited on working people that brought Winnie and George together from their opposing tribes.

They met when Winnie joined the Northern Ireland Labour Party (NILP). According to author Allison Murphy, this radical organisation was a melting pot for Catholics and Protestants to debate together how they could unite workers, leave the sectarian slaughter of recent years behind them and turn Belfast into a socialist paradise.

George was a Protestant from Belfast. He was an Orangeman, ex-member of the Ulster Volunteer Force (UVF) and British Army soldier in World War I. Winnie was a Catholic from Bangor. She'd been a suffragette, a founder member of Belfast's Cumann na mBan (formed to oppose the UVF) and secretary and confidante to James Connolly, leader of the Irish Citizen Army (ICA). She was the first woman to enter the General Post Office in Dublin on that fateful Easter Monday 1916, risking her life to fight the very empire that George was, at the same moment, risking his life to protect.

At meetings of the NILP, Winnie would have listened as George described how he'd left part of his soul at the Somme, when he'd had to kill ordinary working-class boys, just the same as himself. George would have listened as Winnie described how she had refused to leave the wounded Connolly as the GPO burned, and how she'd been haunted by imprisonment and harassment ever since.

Each would have understood that the other had endured losses that separated them from other people and changed them forever. Each worked towards workers' rights and a system that could combat the tide of fascism rising across Europe. They respected their differences; there was so much more uniting them than dividing them.

Not that they always agreed in their debates: Winnie still felt that the martyr-like deaths after the Rising had been essential for the greater good of a workers' republic, whereas George had seen enough of wasteful killing and felt it an abomination in any situation.

Eventually, after not a little persuasion from George, Winnie agreed to get engaged. If like-minded friends were shocked, they didn't show it, although the same could not be said for the Carney and McBride clans, whose vociferous disapproval made Winnie and George determined to do things their way. Leaving their respective families to seethe, they took off by themselves and married in a Welsh registry office. On their return, they moved into 3 Whitewell Parade, Whitewell Road, north Belfast.

Happy ever after?

When she married, Winnie gave up work and arranged for the frail Mrs Carney to move into Whitewell Parade, perhaps taking the place of the children Winnie and George were never to have. To her surprise, Mrs Carney got on famously with her son-in-law. Elsewhere in the family bad feeling persisted: Winnie's brother returned from America furious to discover who and what his brother-in-law was, while George's mother died without reconciling with her son.

In the 1930s, the couple became disillusioned with politics. For Winnie the Irish Free State was not the Ireland Connolly had given his life for, while George was disappointed by the non-appearance of a dynamic movement that could achieve a workers' republic. George was broken-hearted when he realised there was another war coming; the words of the song addressed to a different Willie McBride in 'The Green Fields of France' were coming true:

Well, the sorrow, the suffering, the glory, the pain,
The killing, the dying were all done in vain.
For young Willie McBride it all happened again,
And again, and again, and again, and again.

By now Winnie had become ill with TB, possibly contracted during her prison sentences two decades before. As the Blitzing of Belfast raged around her, she was too unwell to hide anywhere but under the stairs in her own house.

Out of love and pride, George encouraged his wife to seek recognition for the health-wrecking work she had done for Ireland. But by the time she received recognition in the form of her pension as a founding member of Belfast Cumann na mBan, she was terminally ill. She died in 1943 and was buried in Milltown cemetery. George never remarried.

Beneath her placid, almost timid exterior, there burned fires that could scorch.

Obituary, *The Torch* newspaper

In 2016, as part of the island of Ireland's Decade of Centenaries, the medals of Winnie and George – hers from Cumann na mBan, and his from World War I – were displayed together in Belfast City Hall as a 'message of reconciliation'. It was a fitting celebration of the couple who refused to allow politics, family, age or religion to stand in the way of love.

Timeline

4 December 1887 Maria Winifred Carney ('Winnie') born in Bangor, County Down, Northern Ireland

10 February 1898 George McBride born in Belfast, Northern Ireland

1912 Winnie joins Irish Textile Workers' Union as secretary

1913 George joins Ulster Volunteer Force (UVF)

1913 Winnie joins Irish Citizen Army, becoming leader James Connolly's secretary

1914 George joins British Army; serves with Ulster's 36th Division at the battles of the Somme, Messines, Ypres and St Quentin

29 April 1916 Winnie imprisoned in England for her part in Easter Rising; released 24 December 1916

1918 George captured by Germans as prisoner of war; Winnie fights unwinnable seat for Sinn Féin in General Election

1919 George demobbed and becomes an atheist and internationalist

1922 Winnie anti-Treaty during Civil War; imprisoned in Armagh for possession of 'IRA documents', becomes ill and is released

1922–23 Winnie Secretary of Republican Prisoners' Dependents' Fund

1924 Winnie and George meet at a Northern Ireland Labour Party meeting

26 September 1928 Winnie and George marry, Holyhead Registry Office, Wales

1934 Winnie and George attend Wolfe Tone Commemoration in Bodenstown, County Kildare

21 November 1943 Winnie dies, buried in Milltown Cemetery, Belfast

21 April 1988 George dies, buried in Clandeboye Cemetery, Bangor

Grace Kelly about to embark on the ocean liner *Constitution* to marry Prince Rainier, 1956.

Grace Kelly & Prince Rainier

The Grimaldis will never find lasting happiness in love!
Thirteenth-century Monagasque curse

Question: In the lottery of life, what could possibly beat being a rich, beautiful Oscar-winning actress? Answer: Nothing – except perhaps becoming a royal princess.

Such must have been the speculation of Irish-American movie star Grace Kelly when she was invited to a photo-op with the very eligible Prince Rainier III of Monaco.

It was 6 May 1955. Grace had been promoting her latest film *The Country Girl* at the Cannes Film Festival in France. Her studio, MGM, felt that shots of their most famous blonde alongside the playboy prince would garner great publicity. So off went Grace on the train ride from the south of France, along the palm-fringed Mediterranean, to the principality of Monaco, all two square miles of it. It was just another job – but it was a job that would change her life.

At the pink palace Rainier waited. And waited. A power cut at Grace's hotel had challenged the star's hair and wardrobe but, ever the professional, she carried off the unstyled hair and unironed dress with such aplomb, that no one was ever the wiser. With a photographer in tow, the two strolled and chatted, took in the private zoo and smiled photogenically at the sparkling sea view. Grace, wearing the white gloves without which a lady was never seen in public, was coolly professional and pronounced the palace charming. The photos were taken and the two parted – but both dreamt of more from the encounter.

Dark and reasonably good-looking, Rainier might have been a touch shorter than Grace in her heels, but he was an alpha male through and through. Educated at English private schools, he was a decorated WWII soldier, a shrewd businessman and the holder of a seven-hundred-year-old title, which he intended to preserve at all costs.

Neither he nor Grace had had much luck in love up to that point. Grace's directors may have loved the cool beauty and classy demeanour that defined her image, but there was also an aura of suppressed sensuality about her. She had reputedly had affairs with nearly all her male co-stars, single and married, including Clark Gable, Ray Milland, Bing Crosby, and Gary Cooper. Her family were not impressed. They were new money in Philadelphia; Grace Kelly's grandparents had come from near Newport in County Mayo in 1887, and her grandfather and father had worked as bricklayers before making their fortune. Despite the money, sporting triumphs and political clout, they were not wholly acceptable to 1950s so-called WASP society, the American elite that was predominantly Anglo-Saxon in descent, which still looked down on those outside their tribe. Wishing to keep their own noses clean, while rubbing other noses in their success, the Kellys wanted a society matron for a daughter, not a Hollywood femme fatale.

As for Rainier, he laboured under a centuries-old Grimaldi family curse, levelled at a raping and pillaging medieval relative, which was said to forever deny Monaco's royal family happiness in love. Perhaps that is why, by the time he met Grace, he'd become something of a womaniser. But he could be coldly pragmatic when it came to his family name; he finished a ten-year relationship with his pre-Grace girlfriend because the lady wasn't princess material. He had ambitions, other than dynastic, for his tiny realm. He wanted to turn it from a gambling backwater into a celebrity hotspot and tax haven with all the high-end wealth and prestige that entailed. His princess needed to be a Catholic, of good background, with money and, crucially, star quality. It was quite a checklist, and Grace Kelly ticked every box.

After their first meeting, an intense correspondence began between the two. Right from the get-go, the stakes were high – with a prince, there was never going to be any casual encounters or a chance of seeing how things developed. Rainier made his intentions clear: he wanted marriage. Grace was flattered, but initially not so keen. Despite her privileged background, his was an alien world. Her French was adequate but standard, and not the same dialect as spoken in Monaco. The women of the royal family were formidable and less than friendly. She knew her freedom would be curtailed and she'd have to give up a successful career. On the other hand, family pressure was on, Grace wanted a husband and children of her own, and he was a *prince*!

At Christmastime 1955, Rainier made the journey across the Atlantic to meet Grace and the rest of the Kellys at their impressive mansion (now owned by Monaco's reigning prince, Albert). Grace went for long winter walks and talks with Rainier, which for the southern sun-lover must have been a challenge. In due course, an eye-boggling ten-carat diamond ring was produced and the couple became officially engaged.

Before taking the irrevocable step of marriage, Grace was required to jump through a couple of hoops. Firstly, and not unusually in royal circles, she underwent a medical examination to ensure that there was no reason she shouldn't have children. A generation later Britain's Lady Diana Spencer would go through the same ordeal before becoming Princess of Wales. For both Grimaldis and Windsors, this was essential; the continuation of the royal line was the whole point.

Secondly and more controversially, Grace's family were expected to fork out a $2 million dowry – and Jack Kelly Senior was not happy about it. After hard-nosed negotiations on both sides, he agreed to pay $1 million towards the dowry, while Grace stumped up the balance herself. Clearly whatever her equivocations of the previous year, she was now keen to marry Rainier.

It was the 'wedding of the century'. First a civil, then a Catholic ceremony took place over two days in April 1956, as thirty million people across the world watched Grace Kelly become Her Serene

Rainier and Grace with their three children, Caroline, Albert and Stéphanie, Prince's Palace, Monaco, 1966.

Highness Princess Grace of Monaco. In true Hollywood style, MGM not only gifted Grace the wardrobe of beautiful clothes from her final film, *High Society*, but paid for her lace and silk wedding dress, which is now exhibited as a work of art.

Happy ever after?

Grace and Rainier went on to have three children, one of whom, Albert, succeeded his father in 2005. Thus Rainier's dynastic ambitions were fulfilled. As for Grace, she worked hard and did much good in what must have been the most challenging role of her lifetime. She headed up the Monaco Red Cross and a number of international children's charities. In June 1961, during a state visit to Ireland Grace delighted local residents by visiting the old cottage in Drimurla (or Drimilra) townland, near Newport, County Mayo, where her grandfather had been born. Afterwards, she kept in touch with relatives and made two subsequent visits, eventually buying the land with a view to building a house there.

The house was never to be built. The manner of Grace's premature death proved to be as dramatic as her life had been. In 1982 she was driving her teenage daughter Stéphanie to a train station in the mountainous Alpes-Maritimes, when she took a hairpin bend too fast, and crashed over a cliff. Stéphanie survived, but Grace died later in hospital of a brain haemorrhage; it is thought she might have had a stroke at the wheel. She was fifty-two.

The family and the people of Monaco were devastated by

Grace's death and the principality entered the most profound period of mourning it has ever witnessed. Prince Rainier never remarried and is buried beside his wife. Grace Kelly remains an international name, commemorated by stamps, coins, film festivals and academic and sporting awards across Europe and America.

Timeline

1297 Rainier's ancestor, Rainier Grimaldi I, becomes ruler of Monaco, now the world's second-smallest country

31 May 1923 Rainier born at the Prince's Palace, Monaco

12 November 1929, Grace Patricia Kelly born in Philadelphia, USA

1944–45 Rainier sees active service in the Free French Army during World War II

1949 Rainier becomes Sovereign Prince Rainier III, ruler of Monaco

1951 (*Fourteen Hours*) to 1956 (*High Society*) Grace makes eleven films before marrying

1953 Grace nominated for an Oscar and wins a Golden Globe for her role in *Mogambo*

1954 Grace nominated for a BAFTA and wins both Oscar and Golden Globe for her lead in *The Country Girl*

18–19 April 1956 Grace and Rainier marry in Monaco over two days

1957 Caroline born; 1958 son and heir Albert born; 1965 Stéphanie born

1961, 1976 and 1979 Grace visits the Kelly ancestral home near Newport, County Mayo

14 September 1982 Grace dies after a car crash

1984 Princess Grace Irish Library inaugurated in Monaco by Prince Rainier in memory of Grace's Irish roots

6 April 2005 Rainier dies and is buried beside Grace in Saint Nicholas Cathedral, Monaco

Love
Out Loud

In all things born, I knew no stain or fault,
My heart was soft to every flower that grew.

Eva Gore-Booth, 'The Weaver'

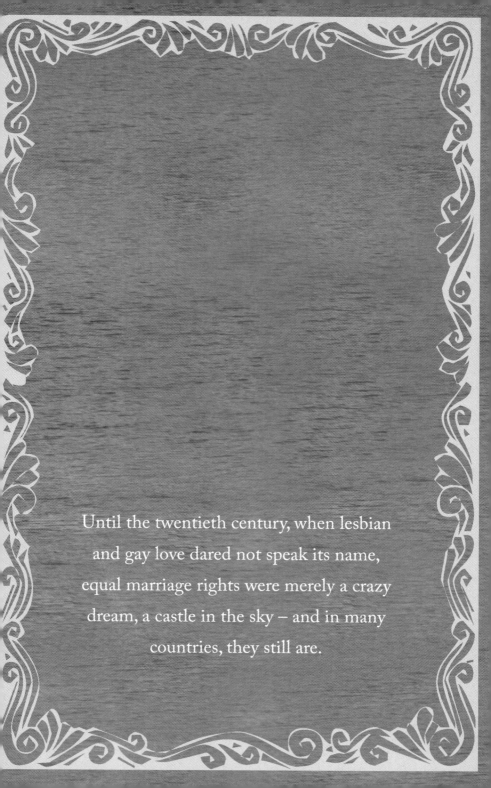

Until the twentieth century, when lesbian and gay love dared not speak its name, equal marriage rights were merely a crazy dream, a castle in the sky – and in many countries, they still are.

An 1850s print of Sarah Ponsonby (left) and Eleanor Butler dressed in riding habits, based on a clandestine portrait of 1828.

Sarah Ponsonby & Eleanor Butler

To preserve [their] retirement from too frequent invasion, [the Ladies] are obliged to be somewhat coy as to accessibility.

Poetical Works of Anna Seward (1810)

Two Georgian women of a genteel class living in a genteel way in a genteel town, the women who were known as the Ladies of Llangollen were celebrated in their own lifetimes for giving up everything to follow their hearts' desires. Fêted they may have been in old age, but in their youth, their illicit love led to a cross-country chase, house imprisonment and exile.

In 1768, Eleanor Charlotte Butler was the twenty-nine-year-old daughter of the House of Ormonde, and Sarah Ponsonby was a fourteen-year-old orphan.

Living at the family seat of Kilkenny Castle, the gregarious and good-looking Eleanor had freedom and energy but not enough to do. Continually batting away one perfectly reasonable marriage proposal after another as if they were flies, her family began to despair. Her interests were not conducive to the job of being a wife and mother, and she read far too many books.

Tall, pale and melancholic, young Sarah's life was harder. Without money, friends or family, after losing her parents, she had been deposited at a local boarding school by her guardian, Lady Fownes.

When Eleanor heard of this through family gossip – Sarah was a distant cousin – she seized the chance to do a good deed and alleviate her boredom at the same time. She visited Sarah at school, encouraged her in her favourite subjects and lent her books from the castle library. Gradually she began to send the carriage more and more often for Sarah to visit the castle. They painted, played music and studied together, mainly philosophy and languages, which both loved.

This happy situation continued for ten years. Slowly they realised that their companionable friendship had turned into romantic love, and that neither could now contemplate life without the other.

But eighteenth-century families could be insistently conventional. Both women were expected to move on from girlish crushes and marry family-approved men. There was literally no place in society for them otherwise – what on earth does one do with a single woman hanging about the house?

Another danger loomed in the shape of Lady Fownes's husband, who was now taking an unhealthy interest in Sarah. The girl needed to be married off smartish, before there was a domestic scandal. Meanwhile, Eleanor's parents were threatening to force their marriage-defying daughter into a French convent.

By the spring of 1778, these events were overtaking Eleanor and Sarah. There was only one option left. They had to elope.

Their first attempt was a farce. One night, they disguised

Kilkenny Castle,
steel engraving, 1842,
after William Henry
Bartlett.

themselves in men's clothes, took two horses and two pistols and headed for Waterford where they planned to take passage for England. They were betrayed and Eleanor's furious father galloped after them, accompanied by the local militia. The women were found hiding in a barn just two miles from the harbour. They were rounded up and dragged back to Kilkenny, where they were locked up at home, and forbidden to see each other or communicate ever again. The embarrassed Butlers accelerated plans for the convent.

At this point, Eleanor and Sarah received some much-needed help from a woman who would become a lifelong friend to both, a servant named Mary Carryl (or Carroll). Acting as a go-between, Mary carried messages and masterminded a second elopement plan.

With Mary's help, Eleanor managed to escape from the castle and make her way into Sarah's house, where she literally hid in a closet in Sarah's bedroom, fed and shielded by Sarah and Mary. After a week of this, Eleanor and Sarah found the strength to emerge. Together they negotiated with the families, who were by now dying of social shame. The families agreed to let them go away together, and even funded the pair with a small allowance of nearly

£300 a year (approximately €60,000 in today's money). There was one condition – that they never, ever return to Kilkenny.

ꙮ Happy ever after?

Once they were together full-time, life became idyllic for Eleanor and Sarah. Together they discovered beautiful North Wales, with its mountains and streams, and moved into a house in the Vale of Llangollen. Here, dressed in masculine style, they renovated, extended and decorated until the original cottage was a crazy Gothic landmark, which can still be seen today. For fifty years, as the faithful Mary waited on them, they landscape-gardened and self-educated, becoming beloved eccentrics along the way. There was a never-ending stream of famous visitors and correspondents. The poets William Wordsworth, Robert Southey and Lord Byron visited, as did essayist Thomas de Quincey, novelists Sir Walter Scott, Sydney Owenson and Madame de Genlis. Scientists, including Charles Darwin, came for tea and intelligent conversation. Aristocrats attended in the shape of Prince Hermann von Pückler-Muskau, the Duke of Gloucester and, their own countryman, the Duke of Wellington (who organised a pension for Sarah). Many others corresponded. All were charmed by the unconventional lifestyle of the Ladies.

Even in their own lifetime, the great and the good obsessed over whether the relationship was sexual or not. True, the 'celebrated Recluses' as Wordsworth called them, shared a bed and had a succession of dogs named Sappho (after a lesbian Greek poet), but were they actually lovers? Many early biographers were insistent that the Ladies were 'impelled by a desire to lead a secluded life of celibacy' (Hicklin, 1847). The landowning Yorkshire lesbian Anne Lister, on the other hand, felt not: 'I cannot help thinking,' she wrote in 1822, 'that surely it was not platonic ...'

As for the Ladies themselves, they weren't telling. Eleanor's private diaries certainly have a lover-like intensity to them when describing the lifestyle of herself and 'Beloved'. But she and Sarah remained private to the end, drawing a protective veil of mystery over their personal happy-ever-after.

> These two ladies ... were so intensely devoted to each other that they made a vow, and kept it, that they would never marry or be separated, but would always live together.
>
> Diarist Mary Elizabeth Lucy

Timeline

11 May 1739 Eleanor Charlotte Butler born, Cambrai, France

1755 Honourable Sarah Ponsonby born, Dublin, Ireland

1768 Eleanor and Sarah meet for the first time

March 1778 First attempt at elopement

April 1778 Second and successful attempt at elopement

1780 Eleanor and Sarah move into Plas Newydd (New Hall), Llangollen, north Wales

1780–1829 Visitors or correspondents of the 'recluses' include royalty, writers and scientists

1809 Mary Carryl dies, Llangollen

2 June 1829 Eleanor dies, Llangollen

9 December 1831 Sarah dies and is buried with Eleanor and Mary at Llangollen's St Collen's Church

Eva Gore-Booth, *c.* 1890s.

Eva Gore-Booth & Esther Roper

Was it not strange that by the tideless sea
The jar and hurry of our lives should cease?
That under olive boughs we found our peace,
And all the world's great song in Italy?

Eva Gore-Booth, 'The Travellers (To EGR)', (1898)

In an Italian guesthouse, in 1896, passers-by might have thought that the two young women standing with their heads together were gossiping. But they would have been wrong. For Eva Gore-Booth and Esther Roper were not chit-chatting about dresses, dances and young men. They were discussing how to change the world.

Eva was pale, fair-haired and, as the poet WB Yeats wrote, gazelle-like; Esther was shorter and darker, with warm, intelligent eyes behind her wire-rimmed pince-nez. They were so different, yet they both experienced their first meeting in the groves of Bordighera, Liguria, as a homecoming.

Eva, the daughter of a baronet (who was also a notable Arctic explorer), had been brought up by governesses and servants at Lissadell House, County Sligo. Esther, the daughter of a factory worker turned missionary, had been reared partly in children's homes in smoky inner-city Manchester. Both were in Liguria for their health: Eva was on holiday with her mother when she came down with a chest infection, while Esther was a working woman on a break from her challenging job.

Esther's father died when she was eight but, unusually, she'd had the benefit of a life-changing education. One of the first women to gain a university degree (First Class), she had for two years been Secretary for the Manchester Society for Women's Suffrage, and was passionately engaged in writing, rallying and organising. Esther, like many Mancunians of the time, was Irish on her mother's side, but she knew few Anglo-Irish people, and she'd certainly never met anyone like Eva before.

Poetic, dreamy and somewhat frail, Eva had been handed her life on a silver platter, yet she retained a burning empathy for those less fortunate than herself. She'd been nine years old when a horrific famine had hit Sligo; watching starving people coming to the Big House for food had marked young Eva forever. Doing ladylike charity, such as needlework classes for the tenants and visiting cottages, wasn't enough for Eva. She needed a bigger job, a useful life, and she knew Esther was the one who could make it happen.

> We spent the days walking and talking on the hillside by the sea. Each was attracted to the work and thoughts of the other, and we soon became friends and companions for life.
>
> Esther Roper, *Poems of Eva Gore-Booth*

Esther Roper, *c.* 1909.

Such was the beginning of a lifelong partnership. The word 'lesbian' was never spoken in public by either.

At the end of the holiday, Eva and Esther returned to their respective homes. Had they admitted to each other that they had fallen in love? We don't know, but Esther did later write that Eva had already decided she was moving to Manchester so they could be together. Back at Lissadell, Eva obviously couldn't stop talking about Esther, whose radicalism started to percolate through the family. Under her influence, Eva and her sister Constance, who later became famous as the revolutionary socialist politician 'Red Countess Markievicz', co-founded the Sligo Women's Suffrage Society.

The following year Eva left Ireland to live with Esther in Rusholme, Manchester. Swapping the majestic views of Ben

Bulben and the Atlantic for the rows of Rusholme terraces may not have been easy, but Eva never looked back. She would live with Esther for the rest of her life.

Happy ever after?

Eva and Esther were lucky romantically and, nearly as importantly, financially. They were able to enjoy independence because Esther brought in a salary and Eva received a regular allowance from the Gore-Booth family (which she spent mainly on socialist and feminist work expenses).

Esther knew that Eva was the one with the charisma so it was she who spoke from platforms all over the north of England about women's and labour rights. They stood up for barmaids, flower girls and pit brow lasses – all members of what we now call the gig economy. They stood up for conscientious objectors in WWI. They stood up for Irish rebels in the Rising, including Eva's sister, Constance. Yeats may have criticised Eva for becoming 'withered, old and skeleton gaunt' because of her causes, but neither she nor Esther cared what he thought. They had each other and their work; they were so close they insisted they were telepathic.

In 1913, because of Eva's weak lungs, they left the smog of Manchester for the slightly less dense smog of London. There they founded *Urania*, a radical feminist magazine, available for limited circulation only. More than a century before Ireland endorsed same-sex marriage by popular vote, this magazine, edited by Eva, celebrated same-sex love and gender fluidity. Eva wrote poems to 'EGR'.

Eva had always been frail and, in the last decade of her life, her health deteriorated sharply. She died in Esther's arms, at the house they shared in Hampstead, North London, and was buried in the nearby St John's churchyard. Afterwards Esther valiantly pushed on and published her partner's poems. When she died, she was buried with Eva under an epitaph from the iconic poet Sappho of Lesbos: 'Life that is Love is God'.

Timeline

4 August 1868 Esther born Lindow, Cheshire, England

22 May 1870 Eva born Lissadell House, County Sligo, Ireland

1896 Eva and Esther meet at Casa Coraggio, Liguria, which belonged to George MacDonald, cleric and author

1898 Eva publishes her first collection, *Poems*

1904 Eva elected to the council of the Manchester and Salford Women's Trades Union Council (MSWTUC) as joint organising secretary; publishes *Unseen Kings*

1907 Esther and Eva distance themselves from the women-only suffrage movement Women's Social and Political Union (WSPU) on pacifist grounds

1907 Eva publishes poems 'Women's Trades on the Embankment' and 'A Lost Opportunity' in *The Egyptian Pillar*

1911 Eva works as a pit brow lass to draw attention to employment rights

1913 Eva and Esther start *Urania*, a privately circulated feminist magazine

1914 Eva and Esther write an open letter to German women, calling for peace

1916 Eva successfully lobbies against Constance's execution; she also unsuccessfully pleads for Roger Casement's life but fails, partly due to his having been outed as gay

30 June 1926 Eva dies of bowel cancer, Hampstead, London

1929 Esther edits *Poems of Eva Gore-Booth*

1934 Esther edits *The Prison Letters of Countess Markievicz*

28 April 1938 Esther dies of heart failure, Hampstead, London

Hilton Edwards (left) and Micheál Mac Liammóir outside
the Gate Theatre, Dublin, 1970s.

Micheál Mac Liammóir & Hilton Edwards

An Irishman and an Englishman have lived together in amity for fifty-one years, have ... disagreed, have agreed again and helped each other ...

Hilton Edwards in RTÉ interview

There may have been play-acting aplenty both on- and offstage in the lives of Hilton Edwards and Micheál Mac Liammóir. But when the two actors first met in Wexford in 1927, they could not have foreseen how much they would each enhance the life of the other – both professionally and personally – and contribute to a country's cultural rebirth at the same time.

It was the summer season, and Micheál was touring with his sister and brother-in-law's theatre company, bestowing Shakespeare on small audiences in 'fit-up' venues across Ireland. At twenty-seven, he was a man at the peak of his beauty. Tall with dark, flashing eyes, black hair and a sonorous actorly voice, he was nothing if not a diva. But he was also a bundle of talents. A skilled painter, linguist, actor, director and all-round glad-hander, he was in love with the theatre, and with Irish culture.

One June day during the run at the Athenaeum, Enniscorthy, a fast hire was required: a young sober actor was urgently needed to replace an old drunk one. Enter twenty-four-year-old Hilton Edwards, hotfoot off the ferry from Wales. As the Athenaeum website records, Hilton and Micheál first met on the stairs at the theatre, as Hilton was going up and Micheál going down.

Hilton was no great looker, with his thinning hair and a remarkably large nose, but he was a serious actor with great stage presence and a fantastic baritone singing voice. He had already appeared in all but two of Shakespeare's plays. Since he was scheduled to play five parts within days, including the role of Iago in *Othello*, the race was on to get him ready. He had to run his lines with someone, and Micheál volunteered for the job. 'The Boys', as they became known, were soon inseparable. At a time when homosexuality was both illegal and taboo in Ireland, the world of the theatre closed around them, offering a safe haven for their relationship to flourish.

To the outside world, Micheál and Hilton shamelessly fictionalised their pasts, especially Micheál. But despite the high-flown claims of a Cambridge degree (Hilton) and a Cork family line (Micheál), the truth was that both were self-invented men from lower-middle class London. They had both been orphaned young, and neither had any assets except not-inconsiderable talent. Hilton had Irish ancestry on his mother's side but identified as English, while Micheál had no Irish ancestry of any description but simply willed himself into being Irish. He was serious about it too – it wasn't everyone who could learn Irish so fluently that he would later write in the language for publication.

In several autobiographies, Micheál outlined the differences between his and Hilton's personalities. He was 'inexcitable', he claims, a laidback man who cared only for languages and the arts and nothing else. Hilton, on the other hand, had an excess of energy. He was interested in everything and obsessed with finding out how things worked.

When they met, both Micheál and Hilton were itching for something meaningful to do. Something big, something splashy, something … well, theatrical. After they moved in together in Harcourt Terrace, Dublin, Hilton came up with the idea that would shape the rest of their lives. They would found a brand-new theatre, and it would specialise in modern European and American plays, the like of which Ireland had never seen before. He originally assumed they would be moving to London to do this, but Micheál was adamant: it would happen in Dublin or not at all.

Happy ever after?

Micheál and Hilton's Gate Theatre started in an annexe of the Abbey Theatre (still run in 1928 by Lady Gregory and WB Yeats) before moving to its own grand Georgian premises. In contrast with the Abbey, which for twenty years had been specialising in Irish drama and dramatists, and spent little on sets and spectacle, the Gate went in for international plays and sophisticated effects.

Hilton was usually the director, and Micheál had his fingerprints all over everything else, from acting to set design to translations.

Because there was now an international offering at the Gate run by two gay men, and Irish plays at the Abbey, Dublin's famously irreverent wits were able to joke that theatre-goers could choose between 'Sodom and Begorrah'. The Gate thrived and among its discoveries were two of the twentieth century's greatest actors, James Mason and Orson Welles who, aged just seventeen, found himself alone in Dublin looking for a job after a bout of mental illness. In 1951 Micheál played Iago in Welles's film adaptation of *Othello*. He kept a gossipy diary about the venture – written originally in Irish for secrecy's sake – to which Welles wrote a fond, witty foreword when it was eventually published.

According to academic Éibhear Walshe in her 1997 book *Sex, Nation and Dissent*, The Boys were at one time 'Ireland's only visible gay couple'. In old age, they became a national treasure, ever-more theatrical, ever-more eccentric, and ever-more adored. Their sometimes tempestuous relationship lasted for the rest of their lives.

Timeline

25 October 1899 Micheál Mac Liammóir born Alfred Willmore in Kensal Green, northwest London

2 February 1903 Hilton Edwards born in Holloway, north London

1917 Micheál abandons Slade Art School and moves to Howth, Ireland, aged eighteen

1928 Micheál directs his own play *Diarmuid agus Gráinne at Taibhdhearc na Gaillimhe*, the new Irish-language theatre in Galway

1928 Micheál and Hilton present *Peer Gynt*, their first production at the Gate

1930 The Gate moves to permanent premises on Parnell Square

1932 Micheál performs in Orson Welles' critically acclaimed *Hamlet*

1946 *All for Hecuba*, Micheál's first memoir (of three)

1960 Micheál writes and performs a hit one-man show, *The Importance of Being Oscar*, based on the life of Oscar Wilde

1961 Hilton appointed head of drama at the new national TV station Telefís Éireann (now RTÉ)

1973 Micheál and Hilton awarded Freedom of Dublin

6 March 1978 Micheál dies in Dublin; Hilton acknowledged as chief mourner by both the President and the Taoiseach of Ireland

18 November 1982 Hilton dies in Dublin; is buried beside Micheál at St Fintan's Cemetery, Sutton

1999 RTÉ documentary *Dear Boy: The Story of Micheál Mac Liammóir* claims Micheál had an affair with General Eoin O'Duffy, leader of Ireland's fascist movement, the Blueshirts

Legendary Lovers

Red Rose, proud Rose, sad Rose of all my days!

Come near me, while I sing the ancient ways …

WB Yeats, 'To the Rose upon the Rood of Time'

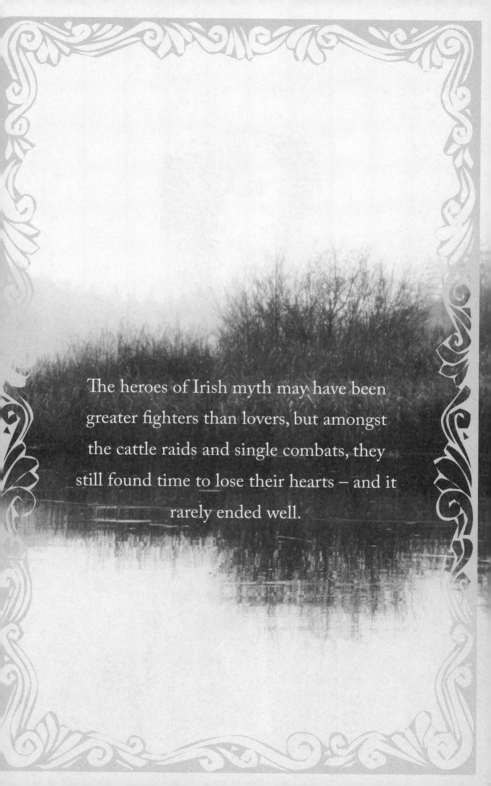

The heroes of Irish myth may have been greater fighters than lovers, but amongst the cattle raids and single combats, they still found time to lose their hearts – and it rarely ended well.

Deirdre of the Sorrows, as played by
Molly Allgood (stage name Máire
O'Neill), 1910.

Deirdre & Naoise

In death her spirit might find its way to the blue hillside
in Scotland and her beloved Naoise.

Eithne Massey, *Legendary Ireland* (2013)

Passion, loyalty, betrayal and revenge – the story of Deirdre and her lover Naoise has it all. Ancient it may be, but its drama centres on that question so beloved of sagas and soap operas alike: what happens when you fall for the wrong person?

Lonely and beautiful, Deirdre has been kept hidden in the mysterious mountains of County Armagh with her foster mother Leabharcham ('Pronounced Laver-cam') on the orders of King Conchobhar of Ulster, who wants to marry her when she's old enough. Deirdre and Leabharcham live contentedly enough until one day, when Leabharcham is skinning a slaughtered calf outside their little house, a black raven swoops down and drinks the red blood trickling onto the white snow. Deirdre, who has never even seen a man, has a sudden clear vision of her future lover – a tall young warrior with raven-black hair, snowy white skin and cheeks as red as blood.

Inconveniently, this description is nothing like old King

Conchobhar, whose hair by this time is not black as a raven's wing, but grey as a goat's rump. Nervously, Leabharcham tells Deirdre that the man of her vision can only be Naoise, the eldest son of Usna, and the greatest warrior in the King's troop.

Naoise is the sort of hero who can run faster than a greyhound and knock out a hundred men with one blow. He is tall, brave, and so generous that he'd give you his head if he had two of them. In short, he is the best man in Ireland by a long shot. Not surprisingly, Deirdre expresses an interest and wants to see him in the flesh. She gets Leabharcham to agree to lure him into the wood with the promise of deer-hunting, so that she can spy on him from behind a tree.

So it is that, one morning, Naoise appears in the woods with his two younger brothers, Ardán and Ainnle. As soon as Deirdre sees him, she is lost. This is the very man of her vision, even more gorgeous in person. As if in a dream, she steps out of her hiding place into a sunny glade. Naoise is struck speechless. As the chief druid Cathbhad had foretold at her birth, Deirdre is so 'fair, comely and bright-haired' that 'heroes will fight for her and kings go seeking her.'

Deirdre and Naoise spend that first magical day falling deeply in love. Deirdre reveals that the doomy druid had also foretold that she would bring the destruction of the King's troop, the Red Branch, of which Naoise is a proud member. Unconcerned, Naoise shows off to Deirdre about how he and his brothers are the best warriors Conchobhar has, and about how he killed the king of

Norway with a magic sword given to him by the sea god.

Once the small talk is over and night falls, they seal their love with their first kiss. By now, Deirdre has already made the decision to run away with Naoise. In fact, in the ancient versions of the tale, it is always Deirdre who takes the lead – no passive Sleeping Beauty, she. Naoise, on the other hand, has serious qualms about betraying Conchobhar, both as a love rival and as his king. According to one version, Deirdre deals with this minor problem by quieting his fears with her loving words. Another version has her rather less sentimentally (but probably more efficiently) putting a spell on him so he is obliged to take her away. Either way, they flee, and the two brothers go too, out of loyalty to Naoise.

> There has never been the like of the joy we'll have, Deirdre, you and I, having our fill of love at the evening and the morning till the sun is high.
>
> JM Synge *Deirdre of the Sorrows*

Predictably enough, King Conchobhar goes crazy with jealous rage when he discovers what has happened. He has waited sixteen years for the beautiful girl to grow old enough to marry and just as he is about to possess his prize, she vanishes. He orders his druids to lay magical traps for the four fugitives, but these all fail, and before long, they are safely across the sea in Scotland.

Several years pass. Deirdre and Naoise have two children whom they foster out to Naoise's friend the sea god. There's one skirmish when the Scottish king decides he too is in love with Deirdre, but they again escape further into the wilderness and out of harm's way to the area today known as Loch Etive. Deirdre couldn't be happier.

But this story is not called Deirdre of the Happiness, and this calm state of affairs does not last. The next twist of the tale sees the appearance of the pure-hearted warrior Fergus Mac Róich, who tracks the exiles down to inform them that all is forgiven and Conchobhar wants them back.

Deirdre is horrified, but the homesick brothers are like three dogs with six tails. They want to rejoin the Red Branch and refuse to listen to Deirdre's nonsense. Fergus guarantees their safety – Conchobhar wouldn't dare harm them while he's around. With a heavy heart, Deirdre follows the jubilant Naoise back to Ireland, crying all the way. She composes a lament, which celebrates her love of Scotland where she has been so happy, but also foretells her doom:

> There is the howling of dogs in my ears; a vision of the night
> is before my eyes; I see Fergus away from us; I see Conchobar
> without mercy in his dun; I see Naoise without strength in
> battle ...
>
> *Cuchulain of Muirthemne*, translated by Lady Gregory

The very first thing that happens when the exiles make landfall is that Fergus is called away to attend a feast. This obviously is the devious doing of King Conchobhar. However, Fergus's son remains and, after all, Conchobhar has given his word that he will not harm them, so the journey continues …

When the guests finally arrive at the guesthouse in Conchobhar's fort, the king is informed (by a panicking Leabharcham) that Deirdre has not worn well and is now a toothless old hag. He sends a spy to the house to check. Peering through the window, the hapless man startles Deirdre in the act of playing chess, where-upon she hurls a chess piece at him and puts his eye out. Bleeding, he runs back to the king, reporting that Deirdre is still so beautiful it was worth losing his eye just to get a look at her.

This news of Deirdre's undiminished loveliness tips Conchobhar completely over the edge and he breaks a major part of the ancient Gaelic code of hospitality: he orders his Red Branch warriors to ambush the guests. Half of the men refuse to do it out of loyalty both to their one-time comrades and to ancient customs, but the other half are soon attacking the house with swords and spears. The doomy prophecy of the bony-fingered druid has started to come true.

There ensues a valiant battle, with the three sons of Usna form-ing a ring around Deirdre and killing dozens of knights with each mighty slash of their swords. Conchobhar sends in his own son to fight Fergus's son in single combat, and they kill each other. It is stalemate, until Conchobhar once again calls upon his druids to intervene.

A dark sea rises on dry land around Deirdre and the sons of

Usna. As the water swirls over their heads, the swords drop out of their hands and they are captured.

Conchobhar knows perfectly well he cannot kill the captives, so he switches to plan B: he calls for a volunteer to do the deed instead. Everyone shuffles and looks at their feet until, from the back of the crowd, one man steps forward. It is Maine Rough Hand, the last remaining son of the king of Norway, and he has a score to settle with Naoise.

At this point, a touching competition arises among the sons of Usna about who should be killed first. Ainnle, the youngest, begs to be killed first so he won't have to live even a moment without his brothers. Ardán begs to be killed first so he won't have to watch his brothers die. Finally, Naoise gives Maine Rough Hand his own magical sword to be used on all three brothers at once. Maine Rough Hand raises his arm and cuts three heads off with one mighty blow. The sons of Usna are dead. And Deirdre is forced to marry King Conchobhar.

Happy ever after

Unlikely, since this is a tragedy after all, and the death of Deirdre's lover is the obvious place to finish it. However, during the hundreds of years when stories were recounted at the fireside, any storyteller worth his or her salt could always string out a good one, and there are several epilogues in this tale.

First off, Fergus Mac Róich eventually gallops in with a major

Loch Etive in the western Scottish Highlands, where Deirdre and Naoise fled.

hangover from his feast, only to find that, not only has Conchobhar dishonoured him and everyone else by having the sons of Usna beheaded, but that his own son is dead. His response is to burn Conchobhar's fort to the ground, and ride off with half the Red Branch warriors to join Conchobhar's enemies in Connacht. This provides neat motivation for another famous Irish epic, the Táin Bo Cuailgne (Battle Raid of Cooley), which features the wicked Queen Maeve, the superhero Cú Chulainn, and some very attractive bulls.

Secondly, all versions of this legend have some variation of events after Deirdre marries Conchobhar. Because what happens when a despot moves heaven and earth to get his own way? The answer is, of course, that everyone ends up miserable, even the despot. Conchobhar lavishes gifts on Deirdre, who refuses to speak to him or even look at him until, finally, in despair he asks her if there is anyone she hates in the world more than he. She names Maine Rough Hand, who killed Naoise. Conchobhar then spitefully hands her over to the Norwegian to do with as he will for a year, forcing her to be 'a ewe between two rams', as he charmingly puts it.

Deirdre shows her independent spirit for the last time. Rather than suffer such a fate, she throws herself from Maine's speeding chariot to her death. In remorse, Conchobhar buries her near Naoise.

To this day, there are placenames that commemorate Deirdre and Naoise and the love they had for each other. According to *The*

Irish Times, local historian John McFarlane has identified many Scottish Gaelic placenames associated with the legend, including Dùn Mhic Uisneachain (Fort of the Sons of Usna), Dùn Mòr/ Dùn Dheurtshuil (Deirdre's Fort, using the ancient spelling of Deirdre, which means 'eyes of sorrow') and Coille Nathais (Naoise's Forest). Across the sea in Northern Ireland, Ballycastle Bay, under Fair Head in Antrim, is said to be where Deirdre and the Sons landed on their return, while Torr Head is believed to be where Fergus abandoned them. The ghosts of Deirdre and Naoise may yet wander these headlands, hills and glens.

Timeline — ⚬⚬⚬⚬

c. Thirteenth century. Earliest existing version of the Deirdre story, known as the Glen Massan manuscript, today held in the National Library of Scotland

1906 Yeats produces his play *Deirdre*

1910 Synge's last play *Deirdre of the Sorrows* staged posthumously

1930 Eva Gore-Booth publishes her protest play *The Buried Life of Deirdre*

Cú Chulainn Courts Emer
by Stephen Reid, 1909.

Emer & Cú Chulainn

[A]nd yet I think it may be proud Emer, Cuchulain's [sic] fitting wife,
who will linger longest in the memory.
What a pure flame burns in her always ...

WB Yeats, Preface to *Cuchulain of Muirthemne* (1902)

An ancient tale that has a higher body count than a Scandi thriller, the Wooing of Emer by the hero Cú Chulainn is a lively combination of improbable feats, sassy women and double entendres.

The story opens in the fort of Emain Macha (today known as Navan Fort, County Armagh) on the day that King Conchobhar and the warriors of Ulster notice that the teenaged hero Cú Chulainn had become rather too attractive to their womenfolk. This startling realisation requires action: Cú Chulainn needs a wife of his own, not just to prevent the ruination of wayward Ulster-women, but also to produce a son, for druids have prophesied that Cú Chulainn will die young.

Cú Chulainn, luxuriating in cast-iron self-esteem, shrugs and announces that of all the maidens of Erin, he will only marry his equal in age, shape, race, skill and deftness. Off go the royal messengers from Emain Macha to every fort in Ireland, only to return after a year and a day, having failed to find a bride.

In the meantime, however, Cú Chulainn takes matters into his own hands. He has heard tell of a beautiful and clever woman named Emer, daughter of Forgall Monach the Cunning. So he dons his purple cloak, purple shield and gold-hilted sword, and off he goes to present himself to the lovely Emer, whom he assumes will fall into his arms at first sight.

In a garden inside Forgall's fort sits Emer with her foster-sisters. She immediately recognises the muscled, young celebrated warrior and stands to exchange greetings.

Emer has all of the six gifts of womanhood necessary to a Celtic chieftain's daughter, i.e. beauty, voice, sweet speech, needle-work, wisdom and chastity. But she is also a woman with high matrimonial standards. Switching to riddles to talk to the hero, she questions him about his intentions.

Cú Chulainn is impressed with Emer's cleverness, but he is even more impressed with her stunning face and form – particularly form. A glimpse of the top of her breasts inflames his passions to bursting point. He would, he replied, lapsing into hopeful double entendre, love to visit the fair country before him. But Emer shakes her head. No man can enter, she replied, until he has killed one hundred men at every ford between her father's fort and Emain Macha.

Undaunted, Cú Chulainn says he yearns to play in the beautiful country in front of him. Never a man will play there, replies Emer, until he accomplishes the feat of the salmon leap while carrying twice his weight in gold, and also strikes down three groups of nine men with a single stroke, leaving the middle man of each nine unharmed.

But still, Cú Chulainn declares, how he would love to lay his head down and rest in the beautiful country before him. It will never happen for any man, replies Emer, until he has gone sleepless from Samhain (31 October), at the turning of the year, until Imbolc (1 February) when the lambs are born; and from Imbolc to Bealtaine (1 May) when the hawthorn blooms.

Beaten, Cú Chulainn limps back to tell his charioteer he is in love with one high-maintenance princess, while the foster-sisters shoot off to inform Forgall that Emer has been talking gobbledegook with a handsome hero, and there is definitely something going on.

For Forgall this is not welcome news. Cú Chulainn's disfiguring and supernatural battle frenzies are infamous and Forgall stonily regards him as nothing but a warped freak. Consequently he asks King Conchobhar to send him away to Scotland for training, as far from his daughter as possible. Cú Chulainn sees Emer just once more before he leaves, and they both promise to preserve their chastity until his return.

After many adventures (including a total lack of chastity-preserving, on the part of the hero, which did lead to problems later), Cú Chulainn returns to Emain Macha where he learns that Forgall is trying to marry Emer off to a local chieftain. He soon finds the hapless man and explains very clearly why marrying Emer would not be good for his health. Having disposed of the opposition, he makes time for many side-adventures by staying awake and fighting from Samhain to Imbolc and from Imbolc to Bealtaine, thereby discharging one of Emer's conditions.

Cú Chulainn now focuses on Forgall's fort, which he attacks by performing his special move, the heroic feat of the salmon leap. He carries off Emer and one foster-sister, each with their load of silver and gold. On his way out, he kills three groups of nine men, sparing only the middle ones – who happen to be Emer's three brothers – and thereby completing another of Emer's conditions. On the way home to Emain Macha Cú Chulainn kills a hundred men at every ford he crosses. He has now completed the last of Emer's conditions.

But the pair are not out of the woods yet. Once they reach Emain Macha, a vicious-tongued courtier reminds King Conchobhar it is his right and duty to spend the wedding night with Emer before she can go to her husband. Cú Chulainn nearly loses his reason when he hears this, but the situation is dealt with by bending the rules. Conchobhar does indeed spend the wedding night in bed with Emer – but the druid Cathbad sleeps between them, thereby ensuring that Emer's virginity is preserved for the husband that had done so much to win it.

And so ends the tale of the Wooing of Emer, handed down in the oral tradition until monks transcribed it. Life for the couple continues in dramatic vein, such as when Emer has to lure Cú

Chulainn back from a fairy woman who has fallen in love with him, but that is, as they say, another story ....

Timeline

c. 300 BC–AD 500 Celtic Iron Age

c. AD 50–100 Setanta (afterwards called Cú Chulainn), son of the god Lugh, born and raised by his mortal mother Deichtire in Muirtheimhne, County Louth, Ireland; Emer born and raised in the fort of her father Forgall the Cunning

c. 1600 Earliest surviving copy of *The Wooing of Emer* (Tochmarc Emire)

1902 *Cuchulain of Muirthemne* published, translated by Lady Gregory

1919 *The Only Jealousy of Emer*, a verse play by WB Yeats; 'Emer's Lament for Cuchulain', translated by Lady Augusta Gregory

Site of Emain Macha, County Armagh.

Maeve & Ailill

A man upon a woman's maintenance

Is what thou art, O Al-yill [sic] ...

Mary A Hutton, *The Táin: An Irish Epic Told in English Verse* (1924)

We've all heard of the feisty Queen Maeve (or Medb) of Connacht from the Ulster Cycle – but how many of us remember her consort, the long-suffering Ailill Mac Máta?

Versions differ in how Maeve and Ailill met, though, in most, Ailill is very much the junior partner to Maeve's Wolf-Queen persona. In one, Maeve is a married woman who fosters Ailill, her sister's grandson. She rears, promotes and eventually, when he is still a teenager, seduces him. Maeve's jealous husband foolishly challenges Ailill to single combat, with the inevitable consequence of his own death. Young Ailill then marries his grand-aunt and becomes king of Connacht.

In another version, less queasy-making in terms of grooming and incest, Ailill is a prince from Leinster and Maeve is the daughter of the High King of Ireland. When it comes to marrying, Maeve demands three things: her husband must be without meanness, without fear and, most of all, without jealousy. The other suitors can manage the first two, but Ailill is the only one who can manage the third.

Had the man, who should win me, jealousy,

It were not fit that we should be together,

Seeing that I was ne'er without a man …

Mary A Hutton, The Táin

In any case, according to legend, they marry and live in Cruachain (today known as Rathcroghan, County Roscommon), the royal seat of Connacht, and they are well-matched. Ailill is a renowned warrior but the majestic Maeve is described as so beautiful that her looks can rob men of two-thirds of their strength. She and Ailill are similarly power-hungry and promiscuous – especially Maeve who seems to have been absolutely insatiable, taking up to thirty lovers a night.

Most accounts of Maeve also mention her implacable hatred of her ex-husband, Conchobhar Mac Nessa, usurper of the Ulster kingship, and serial seducer of Maeve's sisters. So deep is her hatred of Conchobhar that when she and Ailill have had seven sons, Maeve demands that a druid foretell which of them is destined to kill Conchobhar. The druid replies that it is the one named 'Maine', whereupon she calls them all Maine to shorten Conchobhar's odds. (Unfortunately, as is often the way with obscure druidic pronouncements, it doesn't work out as expected: One of the sons, Maine Andoe, does indeed kill a warrior named Conchobhar, but a different one altogether from Maeve's target.)

In the main legend about Maeve and Ailill, we meet the two in bed bickering, as all marrieds do. The dispute is about who is the

MAEVE. QUEEN OF CONNAUGHT.

First Century

Queen Maeve, who ruled from Rathcroghan, County Roscommon.

wealthier. When it turns out to be Ailill, because he has acquired a prize bull that used to belong to Maeve, she demands that he help her invade Ulster and steal another prize bull to even things up. From this lovers' tiff arises the most famous tale in the Ulster Cycle, the Táin Bo Cuailgne (Cattle Raid of Cooley). And the rest is prehistory …

Happy ever after?

In all versions of their life together, Ailill controls his jealousy at his wife's continual unfaithfulness. During the Cattle Raid, when Maeve disappears with Fergus Mac Róich, the ex-king of Ulster, for a night of passion on the campaign trail, Ailill's somewhat Freudian reaction is to steal Fergus's sword and replace it with a wooden one, keeping the real one until Fergus should need it in battle.

But in the end, even Ailill reaches his limit. When he sees Maeve and Fergus bathing together in a lake after the successful Cattle Raid, something snaps. He turns to his brother, who is a crack shot despite being blind, and lays a bet that he can't shoot and kill the creature splashing in the water, which Ailill claims is a deer. The brother takes the bet, lets fly with his spear and kills Fergus instantly.

Maeve's eventual revenge is unsophisticated but effective. When she finds out Ailill is seeing another woman, she urges Conall Cearnach, the foster brother of Cú Chulainn, to kill him. Conall duly follows Ailill to his trysting place and runs him through with a javelin, whereupon Maeve turns on him and announces to all that he has killed Ailill, king of Connacht. Conall is himself then slaughtered by Connachtmen.

Maeve's own violent death takes place many years and many lovers later in Inchcleraun, an island in Lough Ree on the River Shannon. Her nephew, who has vowed revenge on Maeve for murdering his mother, finds an opportunity presents itself while he is having lunch on the shores of the lough. He sees Maeve entering the water for a bathe, and quick-wittedly hurls a cheese at her head, killing her outright.

Timeline

c. 300 BC–AD 500 Celtic Iron Age

c. AD 50–100 Mythical Maeve marches to Ulster in *The Táin*; she is possibly linked with a historical Iron Age queen

c. Eighth to twelfth centuries Monks transcribe stories of *The Táin* for the first time

c. 1160 *The Book of Leinster* contains the earliest written mention of Queen Maeve of Connacht

Sabina & Orwin

Love yet survives though life expires.

National Folklore Collection, University College Dublin

'A Legend of Lough Sheelin'

The sad story of Sabina and Orwin is connected to one of Ireland's oldest castles. But as is usual with ancient stories liberally seasoned, what happened to the lovers is all in the telling ...

Ross Castle in County Cavan (which today does a roaring trade in haunted weekends) dates from the tumultuous sixteenth century. Sabina was the daughter of one Nugent, known as the Black Baron of Ross on account of his black heart. Her lover Orwin was the scion of the neighbouring O'Reilly clan, the sworn enemies of the Baron.

Ross Castle was on confiscated ground, built by the Crown-supporting Black Baron on the ancestral lands of the O'Reillys, hence the enmity between them. Lough Sheelin, over which the castle looks, marked the border between the Crown-dominated territories of Ireland known as the Pale, and the Gaelic-dominated badlands to the north.

Nugent's only daughter Sabina was as good as he was bad. (One local story relates how the Black Baron was so unjust he summarily tried and executed a beggar for theft, not waiting to hear the proof that the man was innocent. The disgusted townsfolk later planted a cross at the spot where the gallows had been.)

Despite being constantly watched by her father, she often used to slip out of the castle to chat to the local people. She loved the lakeshore and sometimes would have her page row her across Lough Sheelin to Church Island so she could walk among the holy ruins.

One day Sabina heard the most beautiful singing floating across the water. She called for her servant and they rowed across to the island to investigate – and discovered the fugitive Orwin hiding from the Black Baron's men among the ruins.

> Starting, he seized his two-edged sword,
> Yet paused to beauty's sovereign power,
> And such light as did the place afford
> Gave light to love in danger's hour.
>
> National Folklore Collection, UCD,
> 'A Legend of Lough Sheelin'

Having retained her head, Sabina then lost her heart to Orwin. Many secret trysts followed, but the lovers knew they were doomed unless they could elope, for the Black Baron would never allow Sabina to marry anyone, let alone a rebellious O'Reilly. They hatched a plot to meet on an appointed night and disappear to a new life together.

When he got wind of his daughter's secret meetings with

Nineteenth-century view of Lough Sheelin, showing Ross Castle in the distance.

Orwin, the Baron's fury was cold and limitless. The best-known version of the tale says that the very night they were to elope, the Baron's henchmen tracked Orwin to Church Island and drowned him in the lough. The Baron then locked Sabina in her room in the castle tower where, looking out over the lake that had taken her lover's life, the wretched girl starved herself to death.

Another version makes the weather the main antagonist of the story, which speaks volumes about what a poor reputation Irish weather has. In this telling, Sabina and Orwin are hit by a freak gale while rowing to freedom across the lough. Orwin drowns straight away while Sabina lingers for three days before awakening, only to die of despair when she hears of her lover's fate.

A long, lovely old local poem has an even more wildly inaccurate version of events. In it, the whole shebang takes place not in the 1540s but in the 1640s, and Orwin is on the run from Cromwellian troops, whom the Baron, of course, supports. In this version, the death of the lovers takes place not because of a vengeful father or unpredictable weather, but because of the hero's highly-strung nature. When Sabina catches cold and takes to her bed for a few days, Orwin assumes she has abandoned him and pines to death on the island. Sabina returns to look for him, but meets only his ghost, pledging to watch over her in life and asking her to bury him at the spot where they first met. He doesn't need to watch over her for long because, after discharging his burial request, Sabina soon dies of a broken heart.

Whichever version you believe, Sabina haunts Ross Castle and

Lough Sheelin to this day, and it is said that visitors have encountered her restless spirit, following her lost love through eternity.

> Now both one lonely grave do fill,
> Each rolling year blooms flowers o'er them,
> And oft time in the dead of night
> Is seen the proud Black Baron's daughter
> By the side of Orwin, gliding bright,
> And roaming o'er Lough Sheelin's water.

National Folklore Collection, UCD, '
A Legend of Lough Sheelin'

Timeline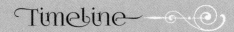

1256 O'Reilly clan become dominant in East Breiffne (modern County Cavan)

c. 1400 O'Reillys command borderlands between Gaelic Ireland to the north and west, and the English Pale to the east

c. 1500 Nugent family start making inroads into O'Reilly territory on behalf of the Crown

1537 Present-day Ross Castle built on a hill overlooking Lough Sheelin (from the Irish Shee-linn, or 'fairy pool')

1566 O'Reilly clan compelled to sign the Treaty of Lough Sheelin with the Earl of Sussex

1601 The last chieftain of the O'Reilly clan is killed; their power collapses

Secrets & Scandals

It is not good to tell a secret to a woman,
but sometimes it may be known through the eyes.
Lady Augusta Gregory, Of Gods and Fighting Men

Elopement, bigamy, adultery –
there are many ways to fall in love and
cause a delicious scandal at the same time,
especially if you live in the public eye.
Some things never change ...

Richard Brinsley Sheridan MP, engraved from a portrait by Joshua Reynolds, 1788–9

Richard Brinsley Sheridan & Eliza Linley

Dry be that tear, be hushed that sigh,

At least I'll love thee till I die ...

Richard Brinsley Sheridan, 'Hush'd be that sigh' (*c.* 1801)

Now a fixture on university literature syllabuses, the dramatist Richard Brinsley Sheridan's early love life was as farcical as one of his plays. In fact, his romantic exploits in pursuing his future wife, Elizabeth 'Eliza' Linley caused the two of them to be splashed all over the scandal sheets of the eighteenth century.

It was 1771 in stylish Bath, a city that was one day to be made famous in fiction by Jane Austen. Twenty-year-old Richard Brinsley Sheridan, a witty and ambitious lad from a penniless but gentlemanly Anglo-Irish background, had moved from Dublin to Bath, to live with his family and to discover what he wanted to do in life. Desperate to keep up appearances, the Sheridans frequented the smartest venue in the city, Bath's Assembly Rooms, where they made the acquaintance of the musical Linleys.

The Linleys were like an early version of the singing Von Trapp family, and their eldest daughter Eliza was a brilliant soprano. Being so talented, she was the family meal ticket, on which her father capitalised by touring her around the country from the age of ten. As well as her fêted voice, Eliza possessed a flawless beauty that dazzled the likes of the artist Thomas Gainsborough, who painted her with dewy lips, pearlescent skin and the requisite two-foot Georgian hairstyle.

> [Eliza Linley's] particular talents as a singer justify the most extravagant description.
>
> *Public Advertiser*, 1770

Eliza's fame brought penalties as well as rewards. She suffered unwanted attention from male fans, including a particularly unpleasant follower named 'Captain' Thomas Mathews, a married man who harassed her constantly.

As Eliza neared marriageable age, her parents felt all their lives would be easier if she enjoyed the protection of a wealthy husband, while they enjoyed a hefty financial compensation for loss of earnings. Therefore, with Eliza's welfare in mind – as well as the family bank balance – Mr Linley contracted her to marry a wealthy man named Walter Long. He was entirely untroubled by the fact that Eliza was nineteen and Mr Long was sixty.

Eliza was horrified. There was a real risk of being committed to the engagement, being essentially the property of her father (who'd already signed the contract). She begged Mr Long to release her and struck lucky. The chivalrous Mr Long not only let her go, but paid Eliza's father for pulling out of the deal. A win-win it might have been for Eliza's father, but Eliza became fodder for a hungry press. A comic play named *The Maid of Bath*, mocking her marital prospects, quickly did the rounds.

This prompted the ghastly Mathews to redouble his efforts to seduce Eliza. Every time her parents were out of earshot, he tried to coerce her to become his mistress, eventually threatening her with rape. Eliza became so distressed she took an overdose of laudanum.

Enter the heroic Richard Brinsley Sheridan, who knew Eliza through his sister Alicia. When she appealed to his honour and informed him Eliza needed rescuing, she found she'd gone to the right man.

Richard had chivalry in abundance, courage and talent too. Common sense, perhaps not so much. But he had quietly loved Eliza Linley for months, unable to declare himself because of the chaos of her public life, the fact that they were both underage and his complete lack of funds. Now, however, was his big moment and Richard sprang into action.

An escape plan was needed to preserve her honour and her life. On the morning of 18 March 1772, Richard pulled up in a carriage and waited outside Eliza's house. Eliza feigned illness in bed until her family had all gone out. She then rose, packed and ran to

Eliza Linley Sheridan, engraved from a portrait by Joshua Reynolds, 1816.

the carriage before the servants noticed. The two rattled out of Bath, bound for Lille, northern France, where Eliza would stay in a convent until the dust settled at home. En route, Richard popped the question. Eliza, caught up in the moment, promptly accepted him.

It wasn't the best-planned elopement. When they got to London, Richard found he had no money for lodgings and had to call door-to-door borrowing from friends. Their ship to France went through such bad weather they both feared for their lives. Outside Calais Richard had to find and bribe a dodgy priest so that they could be married. Once in the convent, Eliza fell ill again, and nearly died.

Throughout, Richard remained a perfect gentleman. He did not attempt to sleep with Eliza – perhaps because he knew in his heart that his marriage was illegal due to the couple being under twenty-one. When Eliza recovered, he unwillingly went home to face the music.

The two irate fathers categorically withheld parental consent to the marriage. Sheridan Senior felt the Linleys were beneath them socially, while Linley Senior felt the Sheridans were beneath them financially. Both fathers were mortified at the massive scandal, which was widely covered in the papers.

But it was about to get worse. When Mr Linley dragged Eliza home from the convent and forced her back on tour to complete contractual obligations, the unpleasant Mathews yet again reared his ugly head. This time he went to the press to defame Eliza, claiming her escapades made her damaged goods. Richard demanded the satisfaction of a gentleman, a duel in Hyde Park, London. The duel was ridiculous – they couldn't find anywhere to fight, one of them broke his sword, and eventually Richard just slapped Mathews about, forced him to apologise in the press and claimed victory. But Mathews soon repented of his grovelling and challenged Richard to a second, more serious duel. This time Richard lost. Stabbed in the throat, he defended Eliza with what he genuinely thought was his last breath.

Richard recovered from his injuries, but his father sent him away to London, in order to split up the young couple for good. It didn't work. When Richard met Eliza again the following year in a Covent Garden theatre, they were both of age, and he wasted no time in asking Linley officially for Eliza's hand. The wedding – formal and public this time – took place in the Anglican church of St Marylebone, London.

Happy ever after?

If the elopement in Bath had caused a stir, married life in London did the same. The Sheridans were gilded and glamorous, but their marriage was tempestuous from the get-go.

Richard's talent as a playwright really took off – hence his appearance on literature syllabuses around the world – but, like many before him, he did not respect the talent that had fallen on him so effortlessly. Like the clown who wants to be Hamlet, instead of being a comic playwright, Richard wanted to be a serious politician. He was obsessed with throwing off what he regarded as the taint of Anglo-Irishness and climbing the greasy pole. It worked to an extent: elected as a Westminster MP, he became famous for his wit and oratory and eventually rubbed shoulders with the Prince Regent himself.

And as for Eliza? A gentleman's wife didn't appear on the stage, so she was unable to continue with her career. But the resourceful Richard charged friends for the privilege of hearing her sing at their homes. From the 1770s he used her other talents too, both as a poet, and as a political hostess from 1780.

Sadly, it turned out Eliza and Richard were not a match made in heaven after all. Both availed themselves of the moral freedom of swinging Georgian London and had affairs. Finally, after they had been married nearly twenty years, Eliza fell for the attractive Irish rebel, Lord Edward FitzGerald. She had a daughter by him, but the pregnancy and birth fatally worsened the TB she'd been battling since before her marriage. She died, aged only thirty-eight, and was buried at Wells Cathedral, Somerset. Richard adopted her daughter by Lord Edward but, aged just eighteen months, the child died and was buried with her mother. Richard remarried three years after Eliza's death.

Timeline

30 October 1751 Richard Brinsley Sheridan born, Dublin, Ireland

c. 4 September 1754 Elizabeth Ann Linley born, Bath, England

c. 1770 Eliza and Richard meet in Bath

1772 Eliza elopes with Richard; Richard fights two duels with Captain Mathews

13 April 1773 Eliza and Richard marry at St Marylebone Church, London

1775 First performance of *The Rivals*

1775 After several miscarriages and a stillbirth, Eliza gives birth to a son, Thomas

1777 First performance of *The School for Scandal*, Drury Lane

1780 Richard elected MP for Stafford, the start of a thirty-two-year parliamentary career

1792 Eliza gives birth to an illegitimate daughter, Mary

28 June 1792, Eliza dies, reportedly at a spa in Bristol; buried in Wells Cathedral, Somerset

1795 Richard marries Hester Jane Ogle, daughter of the Dean of Winchester

1809 Drury Lane Theatre, which Richard co-owns, burns down and ruins him

7 July 1816 Richard dies, London, England

General Andrew Jackson, *c.* 1813.

Rachel Donelson Jackson.

Andrew Jackson & Rachel Donelson

I would rather be a doorkeeper in the house of God,
than live in that palace in Washington.

Rachel Donelson Jackson quoted in
Seven Decades of the Union (1871)

Second-generation Ulsterman and seventh president of the United States of America, Andrew Jackson was, and still is, a controversial figure, with a personality so unbending that they called him Old Hickory after the hardwood tree. It was true to his nature, therefore, that he gave his heart once and forever. The recipient was his wife Rachel Donelson Jackson.

The year was 1789. America had recently won its independence from Britain in the Revolutionary War, and the young republic was building a new future.

Down in the rough frontier settlement known as Nashville, in what would become Tennessee, the circumstances in which Andrew and Rachel met were hardly fairy-tale. Rachel was taking refuge in her mother's compound after five years in an abusive marriage. Penniless Andrew, a war veteran and lawyer, occupied a simple cabin as her mother's tenant.

At twenty-three, they were only four months apart in age. Dark-haired Rachel was kind, warm and down-to-earth. Fiery redhead Jackson was single-minded, hot-tempered and charismatic. On the compound, they became known as a popular, lively couple who loved family parties, dancing and, in Andrew's case, gambling.

Andrew was a lone wolf. From an Ulster Scots background, he'd lost his parents young, and then both his brothers in the Revolutionary War. By contrast, Rachel was part of a large clan who were thriving, mainly due to the fact that they were slave-owners. For Andrew, Rachel was a catch – except for the fact she was already married.

Contemporary news stories vary about how Rachel and her first husband, Lewis Robards (or Roberts), separated. Some say he kicked her out after an affair; others say she ran away because of his unreasonable jealousy. Either way, in the summer of 1789, Robards came to Nashville, where, it was felt by Rachel's family, reconciliation was worth a try …

Except that Rachel did not try very hard, and Robards soon realised he had a rival in the young lawyer, Andrew Jackson. He made the mistake of baiting Andrew to his face and insulting Rachel in graphic terms whereupon Andrew beat him like a dog, and made him run for his life. It would not be the last time Andrew came to blows over Rachel.

Robards disappeared back to Kentucky vowing to divorce

Rachel. What happened next is a muddle. The Jacksons always maintained that, believing Rachel to be divorced, they were married in a Protestant ceremony in Natchez, Mississippi, in 1791. However, there is no record of any such wedding. It's possible that records are lost, but it is equally possible that, driven by passion and the uncertainty of frontier life, the young couple simply grabbed the opportunity to set up as man and wife, a decision that came back to haunt them.

> Heaven will be no heaven to me if I do not meet my wife there.
>
> Attributed to Andrew Jackson

Fast forward four years to late 1793 and to some unwelcome news: Robards had only just completed his application for divorce, citing his former wife's abandonment and adultery. This meant that any Jackson marriage (if there had ever been one) was bigamous. As soon as the divorce paperwork was through in January 1794, the couple quietly married again – this time legally.

Happy ever after?

The Jacksons were a famously devoted couple for the next thirty-four years. Initially living in a log cabin, they bought a cotton plantation and built a grand house, the Hermitage. The Jacksons used enslaved labour to work the plantation and, unsurprisingly, became rich on the back of this. Andrew and Rachel never released any slaves in their lifetime; in fact, the bigger the plantation became, the more slaves they bought.

The Bible-reading, pipe-smoking mother of three adopted children, Rachel was an unlikely femme fatale, but she was never free from the gossip-mongers. Andrew occasionally resorted to violence over his and his wife's reputations, and fought at least one duel, with pistols, in 1806.

Having been both a child soldier and a prisoner in the Revolutionary War, Andrew again took on the British in 1812 and this time his leadership transformed him into a general. Rachel's letters warned him of the evils of life on the campaign trail. She need not have worried; Andrew had eyes for no one but her.

By the 1820s, Andrew was known to all as General Jackson, heroic action man of the people. It was inevitable he would campaign to become US president, which he did twice in 1824 and 1828. For Rachel the campaign was horrific because the 'matrimonial adventures' of the Jacksons were splashed all over the newspapers. *The Phenix [sic] Gazette of Arizona* claimed that Rachel was a serial adulteress, and that previous lovers had paid damages to Robards for 'criminal conversation' i.e. having had sex with his wife.

[Jackson] took away the wife of Lewis Robards and drove him to despair and exile.

Delaware Journal, 1828

The scandal – along with the death of one of her sons – devastated Rachel's health and state of mind. She hid in the shadows as her husband became president-elect in early December 1828, but she never got to witness him taking the oath of office because, on 22 December, Rachel succumbed to heart failure. She was buried in the gown she would have worn to the inaugural ball as First Lady.

Jackson blamed his political opponents for his beloved wife's death and never stopped defending her reputation. The epitaph he wrote for her tomb refers to her as 'a being so gentle and so virtuous, slander might wound but could not dishonor'.

Timeline

15 March 1767 Andrew Jackson born in South Carolina, the only member of his family born outside Ireland

15 June 1767 Rachel Donelson born in Virginia, the daughter of a colonel

c. 1780 Aged thirteen, Andrew becomes a soldier in the Revolutionary War of Independence; is taken prisoner and contracts smallpox

1785 Rachel marries Captain Lewis Robards

1791 Rachel Donelson and Andrew Jackson marry bigamously and set up home

1794 Rachel and Andrew marry legally

1806 Andrew kills Charles Dickenson in a duel; carries a bullet in his own body for the rest his life

1815 Andrew's forces defeat the British in the Battle of New Orleans

1824 Failed bid for the presidency

22 December 1828 Rachel dies; is buried in The Hermitage, near Nashville

4 March 1829 Andrew Jackson sworn in as seventh president of the USA

1830 President Jackson signs the notorious Indian Removal Act, which forces Native Americans from their southern homes to western reservations

1832 President Jackson wins second term by a landslide

8 June 1845 President Jackson dies Nashville, Tennessee

'The Liberator' Daniel O'Connell by Martin Archer Shee, *c.* 1830.

Daniel & Mary O'Connell

You couldn't throw a stick over the workhouse wall
without hitting one of O'Connell's children.

Attributed to WB Yeats speaking in the Seanad, 1926

Handsome, black-haired, and blue-eyed, the twenty-five-year-old Daniel O'Connell whirled through life like a hurricane. Brought up as a young chieftain in Kerry, the man whom George III would dub 'the King of Ireland' was an ambitious young lawyer with a prodigious appetite for work, women and risk. And he took one of the biggest risks of his life when he married his distant cousin, Mary O'Connell.

Mary, then twenty-two, was living a quiet life in Tralee lodgings with her widowed mother, who had eight children on her hands and no income. Mary was attractive rather than classically beautiful, with curly red hair and a cheerful temper, a trait that would be sorely tested in the years to come.

Daniel and Mary met at social gatherings around the county along with dozens of other O'Connell-connected relations. It is not known when they fell in love, but the earliest of the dozens of letters they wrote throughout their lives is dated November 1800, the point at which the two became secretly engaged.

In love letters written throughout their lives, Daniel is effusive in his praise of the 'sweet little woman'. She was his darling, his 'doat', his heart. As for Mary, it is clear she genuinely loved Daniel for his passion, his work ethic and his talent. It's tricky for modern ears, but she often describes herself as 'grateful' to him for making her his wife – a pragmatic view, perhaps, in the face of her limited life choices, and evidence of the dependence of nineteenth-century women on their menfolk.

[Mary] had the sweetest, most heavenly temper and the sweetest breath!

Daniel O'Connell in *Personal Recollections of the late Daniel O'Connell MP*, by William Daunt (1848)

They kept their engagement secret for good reason. The head of the O'Connell clan was Daniel's rich, cantankerous uncle, Maurice 'Hunting Cap' O'Connell of Derrynane Abbey. As far as he was concerned, Daniel was the great hope of his generation, the one who would secure the precarious position of the Catholic O'Connells for all time, safe from the predations of the Crown, which made a habit of confiscating properties, such as Derrynane. He nurtured his favourite nephew, educated him in France, gave him an allowance and made him his heir. In return, Hunting Cap insisted it would be he, and he alone, who chose Daniel's bride. A lot depended on it and he'd already sent out feelers. The lady would

Mary O'Connell with her son Daniel by John Gubbins, *c.* 1817.

have to be Catholic, connected and comfortably off.

Although Mary was a Catholic like her mother, she had inconveniently Protestant brothers. Her surname was excellent but she was the daughter of a mere physician. She was not well-educated or accomplished, and could not speak Irish or French like Daniel's family. But worst of all, Mary would bring nothing with her, except the clothes she stood up in. No land and, shamefully, no dowry.

Through the long months of their secret correspondence, the two weren't even able to meet. Daniel persuaded a cousin to carry the letters, which caused rows when one of Mary more proprietorial brothers noticed how much post she was receiving.

After eighteen months of this, Mary was finally able to see her beloved under the guise of a holiday in Dublin. Daniel, reasoning that asking forgiveness after the event was always easier than seeking permission, seized his chance. On 24 July 1802, a priest married the couple in a quiet ceremony in a Dublin drawing room. Daniel then went back to work and Mary returned to Tralee to her mother.

By now Mary's family had approved the match, but Daniel's family were still in the dark, even his siblings. The 'little woman' turned out to be braver than her husband; she was ready to face down Hunting Cap and didn't care if he disinherited her new husband. But Daniel relied on his position as favourite and was afraid of what the thwarted old man would do. It was only after his visits to Tralee resulted in Mary's first pregnancy that he steeled himself and wrote to his uncle with the shocking news.

Predictably enough, Hunting Cap erupted. On paper, the match was a wasted opportunity that, he felt, would damage the O'Connell family's fortunes for decades to come. He disinherited Daniel immediately, rewriting his will in favour of Daniel's brother, and cancelled Daniel's regular allowance.

Three years into the marriage, Mary was still camping between lodgings and Daniel's parents' home at Carhen, Kerry. The uphill business of winning back Uncle Hunting Cap's favour was taking its time. When their third baby arrived, Daniel recklessly leased a large Dublin house for them all, first in Westland Row and then the very grand Merrion Square. It was here that they finally persuaded Hunting Cap to visit in 1809. Mary charmed him and, shortly afterwards, Daniel was reinstated as his uncle's sole heir.

Happy ever after?

Being married to a hurricane was not easy, as Mary discovered. Daniel ran up ridiculous bills all their lives and, at one point, she had to decamp to France with the children to save money. He was forever agreeing to act as guarantor for poor businessmen, many of whom were relatives that invariably went bankrupt, leaving him saddled with their debts as well as his own.

The most pressing worry for Mary was how to keep her husband alive. As Daniel was a gentleman, he was expected to duel with pistols when he was challenged over a matter of honour – and he was challenged often. When, in 1815, Sir Robert Peel, erstwhile British Prime Minster, challenged Daniel to a duel, Mary put his life ahead of his honour. She contacted a sheriff and had her husband put under house arrest. This extricated him from the obligation, for which he was – eventually – grateful.

Later, his spearheading of the mass crusade for Catholic emancipation would make him the most powerful and popular figure in Ireland, and a real threat to the Westminster government.

> The wily old fox gets around from town to town always surrounded by two hundred thousand men, a bodyguard such as no king can boast of. How much could be achieved if a sensible man possessed O'Connell's popularity, or if O'Connell had a little more sense and a little less egoism and vanity!
>
> Friedrich Engels, *Letters from London* (1848)

Then there were his sexual indiscretions. Daniel had admitted during their engagement that he was already paying maintenance for a 'Mrs Y', whom he had seduced in his youth. But even after their marriage, when he was away working on the country court circuit for up to six months per year, he was not faithful, and Mary received anonymous letters about Daniel's affairs. It wasn't until he rediscovered his religious faith and became the Catholic hero of the nation in the 1820s that he promised Mary he would never again be unfaithful, 'even by a look'. In the 1830s, a woman named Ellen Courtenay claimed he was the father of her adult son, Henry, and the case ended up in court when Henry was attacked by Daniel and Mary's son, John.

This drama contributed to the death of Daniel's 'sweet little woman'. Daniel was utterly bereft without her, especially since he felt he'd contributed to her death. 'I said I would devote my life to making her happy,' the widower tearfully reminisced about their early love affair. 'She gave me thirty-four years of the purest happiness that man ever enjoyed.'

Timeline

6 August 1775 Daniel O'Connell born in Cahersiveen, Kerry

25 September 1778 Mary O'Connell born in Tralee, Kerry

24 July 1802 Mary and Daniel marry

1803–1816 Mary has twelve babies in thirteen years, seven of whom survive to adulthood.

1816 Daniel kills a man named John D'Esterre in a duel; rejects violence for the rest of his life

1825 Daniel inherits Derrynane in County Kerry, which Mary hates

1828 Daniel elected MP for Clare but, as a Catholic, cannot take his seat in the House of Commons

1829 Catholic Emancipation granted

1830 Daniel takes his seat in Parliament, the first Catholic in modern times to be able to do so

1832 A pamphlet is published, *A narrative by Miss Ellen Courtenay, of most extraordinary cruelty, perfidy & depravity, perpetrated against her by Daniel O'Connell, Esq, MP for Kerry* ... in which she accuses him of ruining many women

1834 Daniel brings down the British government over a Coercion Act

31 October 1836 Mary dies, probably of TB, and is buried on Abbey Island, Derrynane, County Kerry

15 May 1847 Daniel dies of a 'softening of the brain' in Genoa, Italy; his heart is sent to Rome and his body buried in Glasnevin Cemetery, Dublin

Friedrich Engels, 1840.

Friedrich Engels & Mary Burns

The Philistines have discovered my life with Mary!
Letter from Friedrich Engels to Karl Marx (1854)

O f all the women featured as lovers in this collection, Mary Burns leaves the least contemporary record – no writing, no portrait, no gravestone. After all, she was working-class, female and Irish, so why would anyone bother remembering her? But remembered or not, it was Mary's love and support that enabled the German philosopher Friedrich Engels to co-develop one of the most influential movements in history – communism.

Friedrich and Mary met in Manchester in early 1843 when he arrived from the Rhineland to work as a manager in the Erman & Engels cotton mill. Energetic and questioning, 'Freddie', as English friends called him, was already a headache for his wealthy family. They wanted him military-trained, Prussian-style, so he could quash rebellious workers when required. Instead, they found him siding with the workers, writing for left-wing magazines and courting arrest. They needed him out of harm's way, preferably in

England, where he could knuckle down to the family business.

It is thought the two might have met in the Salford textiles factory he co-managed, though a somewhat overexcited crony of Friedrich's claimed that they met when Mary was soliciting at the Albert Docks. (This says more about the friend than about her, since the only 'evidence' for this is that she came from a slum). Although Friedrich later complained that '[factory] girls were all short, dumpy and badly formed', Mary clearly did not fit this description being, as Eleanor Marx later described, 'pretty, witty, and altogether charming'.

According to author Roy Whitfield, Mary would have felt more Irish than English. Though born in Manchester, her 'Irish ghetto' circumstances would have given her strong views about the starvation and oppression in her parents' home country. Along with her lively intelligence and trustworthy nature, this was a background that certainly appealed to rebellious Friedrich. The Irish in Manchester had a lot to teach him.

An early Victorian courtship often consisted of long walks and picnics in the country, but the walks Mary and Friedrich took were not like that. Industrial Revolutionary Manchester had become an unregulated, overpopulated, polluted hellhole of untrammelled capitalism. According to official records for the area, in one street in Deansgate, the slum area where Mary was born, there were 'three hundred and eighty persons for one privy'. Infant mortality was so high that the average life expectancy was less than thirty years. It was to this Manchester that Mary introduced her wealthy lover, as she guided him around 'Little Ireland', where, if he'd ventured alone, he might have been picked as clean as a chicken bone. These eye-opening walks and the relationships that sprang from them informed Friedrich's work for the rest of his life. It was said that until the end of his days his favourite meal was Irish stew.

But this was not to be a fairy-tale romance ending at the church altar. Friedrich loved Mary, but his politics and his sense of self-preservation meant he denied her one of the few roles open to a Victorian woman – that of 'wife'. He believed that in wedlock the husband was the capitalist and the wife the enslaved proletariat so he vowed never to marry. In addition, he had to worry about 'appearances'. Politics was one thing, but money was quite another; his family allowance would have disappeared immediately if he'd presented Irish Mary as his wife.

Therefore, though his own circle knew all about Mary, he was obsessive about keeping her a secret from others, hiding their affair from spying colleagues in Manchester and family back in Germany. For most of the next twenty years, Friedrich rented rooms as a smokescreen in the professional district, while living with Mary in different rooms in the worker district.

> I am living with Mary nearly all the time now … I can't dispense with my lodgings [for appearances' sake], otherwise I should move in with her altogether.
>
> Friedrich to Karl Marx (1862)

On the private side of his double life, he and Mary met radical friends and sent regular money to Karl Marx. On the public side, he spent 'party animal' weekends fox-hunting or socialising in his gentleman's club. The best, some might say, of both worlds – at least until Friedrich suffered a breakdown, which lasted a year. What must Mary herself have thought, living in the shadows with no permanent home and no security, not even able to visit her

A cotton mill in Lancashire, England, *c.* 1835.

ailing partner? It was scant comfort to be 'Mrs Engels' only to the tradesmen.

Occasionally Friedrich and Mary travelled. Having witnessed first-hand the influx of evicted famine refugees from Ireland in the late 1840s, they saw the ravaged country for themselves in 1856. We can only imagine what Mary felt in wasted Tipperary, which her parents had left years before in the hope of a better life.

Happy ever after?

In one of Friedrich's many absences abroad, Mary's sister Lizzie moved into their home, and never moved out. Thereafter whenever Friedrich and Mary moved house, which was often, Lizzie went too. From Friedrich's final return to England in 1850 until Mary's death in 1863, the trio kept up an elaborate façade of respectability in a judgemental world.

When Mary died suddenly, probably of a stroke, Friedrich was distraught. He had the only falling-out of his life with his collaborator Karl Marx because of Marx's dismissive attitude to his loss. (Marx's aristocratic wife Jenny von Westphalen had refused to meet Mary, as she was not respectably married.) Marx soon backtracked.

> Mary is dead ... I can't tell you how I feel. The poor girl loved me with all her heart.
>
> Friedrich to Karl Marx (1863)

After the funeral, Lizzie continued to support Friedrich as his housekeeper, and later as his lover. She was both more radical and more determined than her sister. Friedrich described her as 'a real child of the Irish proletariat'. When the pair moved to London in 1870, they lived together openly as a couple, and their home in Regent's Park became a meeting point for socialists.

Lizzie managed something that her sister hadn't been able to

– she got Friedrich to marry her. Unfortunately, as it was the fulfilment of a final wish made from her deathbed, she didn't long enjoy her new status. But unlike her loving, loyal, shadowy sister, Lizzie at least leaves some record of her life. Her married name is inscribed on her gravestone in St Mary's Roman Catholic cemetery in Kensal Green, London.

Timeline

28 November 1820 Friedrich Engels born in Barmen, Rhineland, Germany

c. 1822 Mary Burns born in Manchester, England

6 August 1827 Lydia 'Lizzie' Burns born in Manchester

1842 Friedrich moves to Manchester, to work in the Ermen & Engels Mill

1843 Mary and Friedrich meet, possibly at his mill

1845 Friedrich publishes *Condition of the Working Class in England*

1847 Extended Poor Law passed in Westminster, handing the cost of feeding the famished Irish to their landlords, thus making it tax-efficient to evict families

1848 *Communist Manifesto* published

1849 Friedrich and Karl Marx take part in doomed revolutions in Germany

1856 Mary and Friedrich visit Ireland

1857 Friedrich has a breakdown due to his double life and overwork

7 January 1863 Mary dies in Manchester; her grave is unknown

1869 Lizzie and Friedrich visit Ireland

1870 Friedrich starts to write his *History of Ireland*, but never finishes it

11 September 1878 Lizzie and Friedrich marry, hours before her death

5 August 1895 Friedrich dies; his ashes are scattered off Beachy Head

Charles Stewart Parnell, *c.* 1881.

Charles Stewart Parnell & Katharine O'Shea

Kiss me, sweet Wifie, and I will sleep a little.

Charles Stewart Parnell's final words to Katharine

Unstoppable passion, a vengeful spouse and a bitter ending – all the elements of an eternal triangle are present in the romance of Charles and Katharine Parnell, whose scandalous affair was to have far greater consequences than either participant could ever have imagined.

On a summer's afternoon in the year 1880, the de facto chief of the Irish Party, Charles Stewart Parnell MP, was attending the House of Commons in Westminster when he received a note from a lady. Would Mr Parnell step outside to Palace Yard and have a word with a Mrs O'Shea? Parnell did not know her, but he knew her husband, Captain William ('Willie') O'Shea MP, who was a parliamentary colleague. Courteous by nature, he immediately walked the short distance to the yard to meet Katharine for the first time.

The two chatted for a few minutes and Katharine invited him to dine with her and her husband and some friends. Parnell, a lifelong hater of parties, somehow found himself accepting. As the two shook hands and said goodbye, a rose fell from Katharine's dress. According to Katharine's later memoir, Parnell picked it up, touched it to his lips and placed it in his buttonhole. The rose was found decades later among her possessions, carefully pressed.

At thirty-five, the bearded Parnell was handsome and magnetic, one of the most eligible bachelors in London. He had a high, noble forehead, soulful brown eyes and an enigmatic, aloof manner. He was a mass of contradictions: a Protestant aristocrat who was beloved of the Catholic commoners of Ireland; a landlord who encouraged his own and everyone else's tenants not to pay their rent; a scientist who set up laboratories wherever he lived, yet was so superstitious he was terrified of the number 13 and the colour green.

By 1880 Parnell's star was on the ascendant. He was acknowledged as the leader of the constitutional nationalist movement, Ireland's 'uncrowned king' and ruled the argumentative Irish Party and his increasingly radical Land League with an iron fist. He worked hard in Parliament bringing the plight of evicted tenants to public attention; he was sharp at the political game. But he played his cards close to his chest and allowed no one to get too familiar with him – even close colleagues were not given his home address. The very last thing he was expecting that summer was to fall in love like a schoolboy.

Katharine was also thirty-five and a married mother of three. She was attractive, with a firm, humorous mouth, large nose, luxuriant brown hair and a good figure. She came from a well-placed family with a radical streak; her uncles had been in liberal politics – one was a Lord Chancellor – and her mother was a successful novelist.

When Katharine had been too young to know any better, she had fallen for a dashing officer in the 18th Hussars named Willie O'Shea, whose landowning family were originally from Limerick. Willie's plumed hat, gold braiding and magnificent moustache were all too much for Katharine, and she overlooked the fact that he was a cad and a gambler. Against her father's will, the two began courting when she was only sixteen. After her father's death and as soon as they legally could, they married.

Katharine was now a very different woman from the baronet-vicar's daughter she had once been. She had fallen out of love with her husband and the two lived mainly apart. Yet as a society and political hostess, Katharine still forged alliances for Willie's benefit. The reason she had wanted to meet Parnell in the first place was to advance Willie's political career. The reality was that the O'Sheas had very little money, and Willie needed a boost.

Katharine's dinner party took place followed by a trip to the Gaiety Theatre, where it was noted Parnell spent most of the evening talking to his hostess rather than to Willie. A lunch party followed, then another dinner. Within two weeks of their first meeting, Parnell was writing to Katharine from Ireland, flirtatiously hinting how much he was looking forward to seeing her again.

Katharine took to visiting the Ladies Gallery in the House of Commons to listen to Parnell speak. Afterwards the two had tea or dinner together before Katharine took a cab home to Eltham. The meetings became more private. The letters between 'Queenie' and her 'King', as they called themselves, became more frequent. At some point during the autumn of 1880, Katharine and Parnell became lovers.

Frustratingly for Parnell, their meetings had to take place around Katharine's many commitments. Apart from her three children, Katharine's main responsibility was her rich Aunt Ben whom she looked after in return for a home named Wonersh Lodge in Eltham, Surrey. Katharine would come into a substantial inheritance in due course – but only so long as the O'Sheas stayed on Aunt's good side.

Katharine and Charles knew they were risking much. If they were discovered, Katharine would lose her children, her home and her inheritance, and Parnell would lose his career. In the end, much more even than that was lost – the chance for Ireland to gain a measure of independence when it had been within reach. But that was in the dark future; for now, Katharine and Parnell made the most of their time together.

Willie O'Shea kept to his flat in London, but he had full knowledge of Parnell's visits to Eltham. By the summer of 1881 Katharine was pregnant with Parnell's child. She gave birth in February 1882 but sadly the baby girl lived only a few weeks. It's hard to understand, but Parnell and Katharine managed to keep their distress secret, and Parnell was not even able to attend the funeral of his first child. On top of it all, shortly after the baby's funeral, he was imprisoned for six months in Kilmainham Gaol, Dublin, because of his support for an Irish rent boycott.

Katharine would go on to have two more daughters by Parnell. These two, like the first, bore the name O'Shea. The public, the Irish Parliamentary Party, the aged aunt and the newspapers all remained ignorant of the true state of affairs.

> Parnell and I were one, without scruple, without fear, and without remorse.
>
> Katharine O'Shea Parnell, *Charles Stewart Parnell*

How much did Willie know? Was he, as Gladstone believed, totally deceived, thinking his wife's friendship with his boss to be platonic? Or did he, as Churchill later claimed, accept the situation for the sake of political and financial ambition?

By 1887 Parnell was at the peak of his career, heavily influencing Prime Minister Gladstone's commitment to Irish land rights and Home Rule – and it was Katharine who acted as their discreet go-between. When in 1888 and '89, Parnell successfully saw off, in court, an accusation published in *The Times* that he was complicit in the Phoenix Park assassinations, he was welcomed back to the House of Commons with a standing ovation.

However, by now there was gossip, and Willie was beginning to feel foolish. He took to arriving unexpectedly at Eltham hoping to confront Parnell. Katharine and Parnell leased a succession of houses in Brighton, Eastbourne and elsewhere – under assumed names, of course, the better to avoid him and keep ahead of the press.

In May 1889, Aunt Ben died, and her will, which left nearly everything to Katharine, was contested by Katharine's siblings. Willie O'Shea finally realised that there would not be any inheritance money coming his way after all. On Christmas Eve 1889, he filed for divorce on the grounds of Katharine's adultery, and named Charles Stewart Parnell as his wife's lover.

The effect of this was cataclysmic. A divorce was a truly awful stain on an upper-class family, and placed the participants outside normal society. Married aristocrats were adept at living separate lives and having discreet love affairs, all in order to keep face and to retain land and wealth in the family. On the rare occasions when an estranged couple did go public and divorce, the husband usually did the chivalrous thing, and allowed himself to be caught committing adultery – often in a seaside hotel. Thus his wife, the mother of his children, could divorce him for adultery, and ensure her reputation remained intact.

But Willie was not willing to do the chivalrous thing. In fury he dragged Katharine through a two-day trial in November 1890. It laid bare every deception of the previous ten years, painting the lovers in the most sordid light possible. Claims and counterclaims got messy. Willie claimed Katharine was not only a deceiver, but an unfit mother. He sued for full custody (which he was awarded though he never took it up). Katharine claimed that Willie was an

Katharine Parnell, 1891.

absconder and serial adulterer, on at least one occasion with her own sister. The divorce went through.

The scandal hit the other side of the Atlantic, where newspapers accused Parnell of everything from having an affair with Katharine's daughter to being a bigamist. *The New York Tribune* of 16 November 1890 claimed that, in Brighton, Parnell had had to jump out of a window, and climb down a rope ladder when he heard O'Shea at the front door.

It was not good PR for a senior parliamentarian, but Parnell was serenely unconcerned. He wanted only for the divorce to be over so he could marry Katharine. After waiting so long, he was convinced that his people in Parliament and in Ireland would stand behind him.

But when Gladstone realised that backing Parnell would lose him the support of the Liberal Party – and therefore the next general election – Parnell's once-unassailable position as leader of the Irish Party was fatally weakened. By now committed to Home Rule, Gladstone refused to jeopardise its chance because of the embarrassment of Parnell's affair (which he called 'the sin of Tristan with Iseult'). He required Parnell's resignation.

Haughty, passionate and proud, Parnell refused and told Katharine he would rather die than give in. The Irish Parliamentary Party split, only a minority of MPs staying loyal to Parnell. Some cities, such as Dublin and Cork also stayed loyal, but in other regions, the devotion turned to hatred. In the North Sligo and Carlow by-elections, people said that Parnell was a hypocrite, that he was never fully behind land reform and Home Rule, being a landlord himself. He was too urban, too Unionist, too Protestant, not radical enough and not Irish enough. He did not understand working men and women. Parnell's candidates were trounced by anti-Parnellites.

It was horrendous for Katharine. It was now that the anti-Parnellites took to calling her 'Kitty', a name that, in the nineteenth century, was often slang for a prostitute. They made lewd jokes in the press, one MP calling her the 'mistress of the party'. The death knell for Parnell's career came when the Catholic bishops, having kept quiet until they could see which way the tide was running, went public with their condemnation and demanded Irish Catholics reject Parnell on the grounds of immorality.

On the divorce being granted, Parnell paid £3500 in costs, a huge sum. Then, pursued by the press, he and Katharine were married in a registry office in Steyning, West Sussex.

Happy ever after?

Parnell continued to work feverishly with the few remnants of the party that stuck by him, such as John Redmond, but he was overtaken by worsening health. Four months after he married Katharine, he died in her arms at their home in Brighton. His body was buried in Glasnevin Cemetery, Dublin, under a block of Wicklow granite bearing the single word 'Parnell'.

After his death Parnell was regarded as a major loss. According to Churchill, he would have become Ireland's first prime minister in a devolved parliament, and so much of Ireland's history would have panned out differently. But with his early death the cause of Home Rule took a back seat for another generation.

For Katharine, her love for Parnell forever changed the way she lived her life. Controversy continued to rage around her role in the life of Ireland's lost leader, and she lived in seclusion. Her children were forced to defend her good name – it was reported that her son Gerard once knocked down a man who had spoken disrespectfully of his mother.

'Avondale', a traditional ballad, compares the betrayed Parnell to Jesus:

> Where pride and ancient glory fade,
> Such was the land where he was laid,
> Like Christ was thirty pieces paid,
> For Avondale's proud eagle.
>
> Long years that green and lovely glade,
> Have lost for now our grandest Gael,
> And cursed the land that has betrayed
> Our Avondale's proud eagle.

Timeline

27 June 1846 Charles Stewart Parnell born, Avondale, County Wicklow

30 January 1846 Katharine Wood born, Braintree, Essex

1867 Katharine and Willie O'Shea marry; they have three children

1869 Parnell rusticated from Cambridge for fighting

1875 Katharine and O'Shea separate

1879 Parnell elected president of the newly founded Irish National Land League

1882 Parnell negotiates the Kilmainham Treaty with Gladstone, in which he rejects violence

1882 A daughter born to Katharine and Parnell but dies

1882 Two senior British officials assassinated in Phoenix Park, Dublin

1883 and 1884 Two more daughters born to Katharine and Parnell, and acknowledged by Willie O'Shea

1886 Gladstone's First Home Rule Bill defeated

1889 Parnell exonerated of complicity in Phoenix Park murders

1889 O'Shea files for divorce, citing Parnell

25 June 1891 Katharine and Parnell marry

6 October 1891 Parnell dies of pneumonia, just four months after his wedding; Katharine publicly refutes reports that he committed suicide

1893 Second Home Rule Bill passes in the House of Commons but is defeated in the House of Lords

1914 Katharine publishes *Charles Stewart Parnell: His Love Story and Political Life*

5 February 1921 Katharine dies in Hove and is buried in Littlehampton, England

1912-14 Third Home Rule Bill is introduced and passed but is never brought into force

Elizabeth Bowen.

Elizabeth Bowen & Charles Ritchie

[Elizabeth] was an artist, even in love, fighting for love's survival.

Victoria Glendinning, *Love's Civil War* (2008)

It was Blitz-torn Britain, 1941. Anglo-Irish novelist Elizabeth, forty, was successful and married, and Canadian diplomat Charles, thirty-three, was attractive and single. As so many did in wartime, they may have embarked on their affair as an alcohol-fuelled fling to help them get through the grim nights, but in fact, it was a fling that would last more than thirty years.

In his diaries, Charles recorded his impressions on first meeting Elizabeth, who was then the centre of Oxford and London literary circles. He noted her handsome face with its 'cruel, witty mouth'. He found her intelligent, of course, but also mysterious and poetic. He claimed she had the most beautiful body he had ever seen. Balding and bespectacled as Charles was, he had a distinct weakness for what he described as 'sex excesses', and was apparently irresistably charming.

It certainly wasn't Elizabeth's first affair during her companionable but unconsummated marriage to her husband, Alan Cameron. Cutting a figure as rather a grande dame, she always struggled to balance the life of the mind with her sensual needs. Her formal manners and cut-glass accent belied a romantic centre, and she was attracted to both men and women.

When they became lovers after a trip to see the roses in Regent's Park, Charles felt excitement and pride but also fear – fear she would fall in love with him (which she did), fear she would fillet him and put him in her stories (which she did), fear they would not be able to live without each other (which they couldn't).

They both led frantic lives: one minute Charles might be seeing George VI at Buckingham Palace, the next digging Londoners out of rubble during an air raid. Elizabeth took her turn fire-watching and made what she called 'intelligence forays' to Ireland, i.e. checking on what neutral Ireland was up to for the Ministry of Information in London. One of her best novels, *The Heat of the Day*, is regarded as a masterpiece in its depiction of the Blitz of World War II. It is dedicated to Charles Ritchie.

In public, upper lips remained rigid and proprieties were observed. They met at Elizabeth's 'at-homes' in Clarence Terrace, where Charles would be welcomed by Elizabeth's husband. They met at the Ritz, Claridge's, Kew Gardens and at well-heeled dinners, shows and house parties with friends. Charles visited Bowen's Court, Elizabeth's ancestral home in County Cork. In between, they somehow found time to squeeze in afternoons of sex and conversation in Charles's London flat.

Charles Ritchie talking to President John F Kennedy, 25 May 1962.

What was it that bound Elizabeth and Charles so close? According to biographer Victoria Glendinning in *Love's Civil War* (2010), both felt they were self-made citizens of nowhere, she because she was rooted in the dying Anglo-Irish world of the Big House, and he because he was a professional globetrotter. Each had a biting intelligence, and each provided a unique honesty to the other. He was, as his niece recalled, 'the man everyone wanted to have at their party – the most amusing man you could meet'.

In 1945, Charles was posted back to Canada, and that is where the affair might have ended. But instead it became that painful business known as long-distance love. Lyrical letter writing and luxurious holidays had to serve. Even as their physical affair fizzled out, each remained in love with the other's brain. They were never more alive than when they were together.

Seven years into the relationship, Charles dropped a bombshell: he was getting married, as diplomats generally did. Elizabeth couldn't do anything about it – after all, she was still married to Alan. According to Glendinning, 'her loyalty to the institution of marriage [did] not include Charles's'. She high-handedly maintained that it wouldn't affect their own extraordinary love, and persisted in believing they would one day be together.

Emotional turmoil for all parties ensued. Charles could never decide whom he loved more: his bride, Sylvia, who was like a 'second self', or the mesmerising Elizabeth. Striving to make the two women friends only succeeded in torturing both. Somehow he found time to be unfaithful to both with other women.

Happy ever after?

The author of thirteen novels, as well as ghost tales, short stories and essays, Elizabeth was acknowledged as one of the great writers of the Anglo-Irish tradition. She remained in demand as a lecturer leading a cultured, sometimes glamorous life.

But when dependable, supportive Alan died, the power balance shifted. Elizabeth became very lonely. In 1959, she suffered a nervous breakdown and financial hardship, and she had to sell her beloved Bowen's Court, which she had always regarded as hers and Charles's real home. (In 1961 it was demolished.) The illusion that she and Charles would one day live together was vanishing. Meanwhile, Charles scaled the heights of his career with important postings in West Germany, the USA and Britain.

In 1972, Elizabeth lost her voice and Charles paid for a specialist, who diagnosed terminal lung cancer. Charles rushed to be by her side and came away from their last meeting carrying a poem she'd written for him. She died soon after.

She was buried in St Colman's churchyard, near the site of Bowen's Court. The funeral procession entered the churchyard through the private Bowen family entrance, which, as Elizabeth was the last of the Bowens, was then bricked up. Charles spent his retirement publishing frank and well-received diaries, and died in Canada at the ripe old age of eighty-eight.

Timeline

7 June 1899 Elizabeth Bowen born Dublin, Ireland

23 September 1906 Charles Ritchie born Halifax, Nova Scotia, Canada

1923 Elizabeth marries Alan Cameron

1930 Elizabeth inherits Bowen's Court, an Anglo-Irish mansion near Mitchelstown, County Cork

1937 Elizabeth made a member of the Irish Academy of Letters

1938 *The Death of the Heart* published

1941 Elizabeth and Charles meet and start an affair

1942 *Bowen's Court*, a history of the house, published

1948 Charles marries Sylvia, his second cousin

1949 *The Heat of the Day* published and dedicated to Charles; Elizabeth awarded a CBE

1952 Elizabeth is widowed

1954–58 Charles is Canadian ambassador to West Germany

1959 Elizabeth forced to sell Bowen's Court

1962–66 Charles is Canadian ambassador to the United States

1967–71 Charles is Canadian High Commissioner to United Kingdom

22 February 1973 Elizabeth dies in London; buried, with her husband, Alan, at Farahy, near Bowen's Court, County Cork

1974 Charles's diary *The Siren Years: A Canadian Diplomat Abroad 1937-1945* published

7 June 1995 Charles dies in Ottawa, Canada

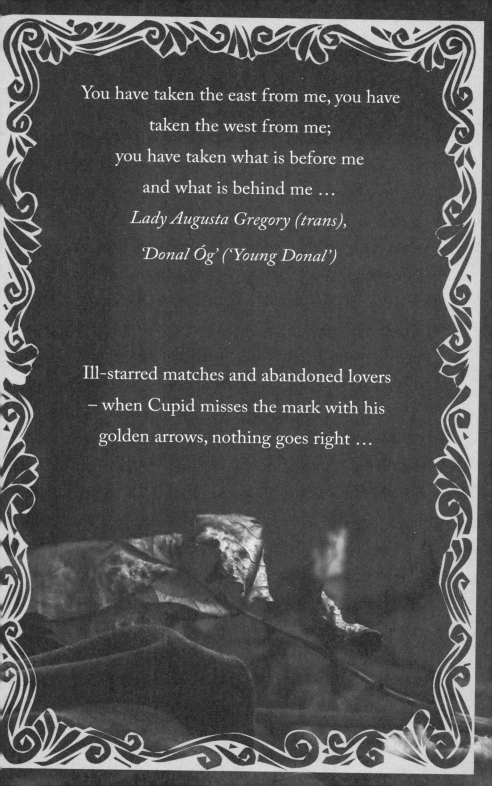

You have taken the east from me, you have
taken the west from me;
you have taken what is before me
and what is behind me …

Lady Augusta Gregory (trans),

'Donal Óg' ('Young Donal')

Ill-starred matches and abandoned lovers
– when Cupid misses the mark with his
golden arrows, nothing goes right …

Reconstruction of a
wooden gallows, used
for executions until the
twentieth century.

Mary Anne Knox & John McNaghten

Nature, to [Mary Anne's] misfortune, had eminently endowed her with amiable qualities of mind, and beauty of person.

Anonymous account of the murder of Miss MA Knox (1762)

The tragic tale of Mary Anne Knox, a teenage heiress in eighteenth-century Ireland, was written up at the time as a love story gone wrong – but the further one gets into it, the less romantic it sounds.

The ranks of Ascendancy Ireland had its fair share of what one might charitably call colourful characters. One of these was a rake who went down in history as John 'Half-Hanged' McNaghten (or McNaughten).

The man was a gambling addict who by the time he met the fifteen-year-old Mary Anne Knox had already run through his own inheritance trying to keep up with the Dublin Castle set. His pregnant wife had died during a visit from the bailiffs, and then he'd lost his government job as a tax collector due to embezzling. He was now penniless and dodging prison, but he had impressed Mary

Anne's father, Andrew Knox MP, as a gentleman down on his luck. He was invited to the family pile, Prehen House, outside Derry.

The romantic re-telling of the tale has it that Mary Anne fell in love with the charming McNaghten, but that the two were torn apart by Mr Knox. However, a more realistic contemporary report claims that McNaghten set his sights on sheltered Mary Anne when he realised that she would bring a whopping dowry of £6000.

He asked her father for her hand and was soundly rejected. Somehow he managed to persuade Mr Knox that, as a gentleman, he would drop the matter. The very opposite was true; he pursued Mary Anne relentlessly. One day, in a quiet part of the house, the girl found herself alone in a room with McNaghten, a witness and a Bible, taking part in a bogus wedding ceremony.

> With an air of sprightly raillery [he pulled] out a prayer book. He began to read the marriage service and insisted on the lady's making the responses, which she did, but to every one, she added 'provided her father consented'.
>
> Peter Burke, *Celebrated Trials connected with the Upper Classes in the Relations of Private Life* (1851)

According to one anonymous account from 1762, McNaghten was allowed to accompany Mary Anne on a journey to Ards, staying overnight at Strabane, in the house of a family friend named McCausland. But when McNaghten attempted to claim his supposed conjugal rights as Mary Anne's husband McCausland raised the alarm and had Mary Anne escorted home. Mr Knox took swift action, barring McNaghten access to Prehen, then legally dissolving the marriage claim in the Irish Court of Delegates, his daughter being underage. McNaghten went to the newspapers, insisting that Mary Anne was his legal wife. It is at this point the story gets even darker.

Eighteenth-century Ireland saw an upsurge in the abduction and forced marriage of well-to-do women and girls that reached almost epidemic proportions. There were even 'abduction clubs' in which a group of men – generally the younger, poorer sons of wealthy families – would toss a coin for some unfortunate young woman. They would then aid and abet each other in kidnapping her. The woman would be spirited away to an inn in the nearest big city, where she would find a bribed clergyman waiting. A wedding ceremony would take place. Once wedded and bedded, the abducting bridegroom would rely on the fact that the woman's family would go along with it, rather than risk a court case, and the social embarrassment of a 'ruined' daughter no one else would marry.

It was about as far from a love story as it was possible to get, but such was McNaghten's cold-blooded plan.

One night, in November 1761, Mary Anne was travelling to Dublin with her parents and two servants for the opening of Parliament. As they drew near Cloghcor Wood, Strabane, McNaghten and three accomplices leapt in front of the carriage and stopped it at gunpoint. They wrenched open the door and attempted to pull Mary Anne out. But Mary Anne's father drew his own pistol. In the chaotic struggle that followed, McNaghten discharged his gun – and shot Mary Anne in the chest. Some reports say she had flung herself in front of her father to protect him. She was carried to a cottage by the side of the road, where she bled to death.

McNaghten's attempts at escape were futile. There was a bounty on his head – the Strabane Historical Society reports it was a hefty one hundred guineas – and he was soon captured. It is recorded that McNaghten showed no remorse for the death of the girl he was supposed to have loved.

At Lifford Courthouse, County Donegal, McNaghten was tried, not for abduction but for murder. He was convicted and sentenced to hang, which is where history and myth collide. When the moment of reckoning arrived, the trapdoor of the gallows opened and McNaghten plunged through – only to have the rope break.

It was believed by many that if a condemned man survived a hanging, he was allowed to go free. But McNaghten apparently shouted, 'I will not be known as the half-hanged man!' choosing instead to re-ascend the gallows. This time the rope did its job.

Now by that name he's known to men,
His half-hanged ghost roams down Prehen,
On moonlit nights you'll hear him cry,
'On the gallows tree, hang me high'.

Bizarrely, in folklore and traditional music John McNaghten is seen as a romantic young hero whose lover died by a tragic mistake, rather than the gambler, gold-digger and would-be kidnapper that he really was.

Timeline

c. 1722 John McNaghten born Benvarden, County Antrim, Ireland
1746 Mary Anne Knox born Prehen House, County Derry, Ireland
10 November 1761 Mary Anne shot and killed by McNaghten
15 December 1761 John McNaghten hanged along with one accomplice
1774 Mary Anne's brother inherits Prehen; subsequently names daughter after his dead sister

Painted by J. Hoppner Portrait Painter
to his R.H. the Prince of Wales

Engraved by J. Jones Engraver Extraordinary to his R.H. the
Prince of Wales, and Principal Engraver to his H.H. the Duke of York.

M^{RS} JORDAN in the Character of HYPOLITA.

To her Grace the Dutchess of Devonshire this PRINT is most humbly Dedicated by her Grace's most obed.^t humble Servt

John Jones.

Publish'd as the Act directs March 1.791 by J. Jones. N.º 75 Great Portland Street.

Dora Jordan as Hypolita, Queen of the Amazons, engraved from a portrait by
John Hoppner RA, 1791.

Dora Jordan & the Duke of Clarence

*[Dora's] smile had the effect of sunshine and her laugh
did one good to hear it.*

Critic and essayist William Hazlitt, quoted in
The Life of Mrs Jordan (1831)

Waterford comedy actress Dora Jordan (originally Bland) was born just about as far from royalty as it was possible to get. But treading the boards in Regency-era London brought her into contact with creatures of every stripe, including HRH Prince William, son of George III, and third in line to England's throne.

Portraits of Dora show a kind and expressive face with an elfin, pointy chin. According to the essayist William Hazlitt, as a personality she was charming, full of 'gaiety, openness and good nature'. She was a great singer and a hard worker.

The jowly, pop-eyed Duke was a naval officer, occasionally lampooned in the press as 'Silly Billy', who lived like the proverbial sailor on shore leave when he was in England. He ate a lot, drank a lot and slept around. As a third royal son, he was not expected to accede to the throne, and was ignored and kept short of funds as a result.

By the time they met, Dora was topping the bill at Drury Lane, but she had been serially unlucky in love. Pregnant and unprotected, she'd had to leave Ireland in a hurry to escape a violent and blackmailing seducer, a theatre manager named Daly. As early biographer James Boaden asked, 'who would have believed in the virtuous resistance of an actress?' In England, she'd fallen deeply in love with a man named Ford, resulting in more pregnancies – but still no wedding ring. A high-status patron was the best she could expect.

Dora and the Duke were introduced about 1790, and both understood the transactional element. But soon the Duke found there was more to it than that. Dora was warm and affectionate, already a maternal figure at twenty-eight, who could give him the love he'd never had.

It seems they had something profound in common: Both came from large, troubled families and craved a happy domestic life. Dora's father had abandoned his family, and left them to scrape a living, which was how Dora ended up on the stage. William's parents had produced fifteen children – most of whom were locked in a power struggle. He was a 'kidult', tied to the royal apron strings, bound by chilly rules and strict protocol whatever he did.

Within a year of their first meeting, Dora was spending every night with the prince, much to the delight of the press who charmingly depicted her as the prince's chamber pot. She faced a hard choice about the three daughters from her previous relationships. She couldn't keep them with her if she wished to live with the Duke, so she awarded custody and maintenance to her sister Hester in Brompton, London. So cruelly was she vilified in the press for 'abandoning' her children that she had to make an impassioned public appeal from the Drury Lane stage.

This now left the way clear for a phenomenal baby factory to go into production, as Dora and the Duke created their own family, and the home life that neither had ever known. In the thirteen years from 1794, Dora gave birth ten times. Although illegitimate, the babies were all given the surname FitzClarence after their father's title. He lived with them full-time.

> [The Duke] is an example for half the husbands and fathers in the world, the best of masters, and the most firm and generous of friends.
>
> Letter from Dora to an unknown friend (*c.* 1809)

Their settled relationship was even recognised by the King, who donated an estate named Bushy Park, near London, for the growing family to live in. Astonishingly, ready cash was so scarce for the Duke that Dora carried on working, and bailed him out regularly.

Dora and the Duke lived happily for more than twenty years, and the Duke was faithful throughout. Dora preserved her good looks, but it was her nature – kind, accepting and possibly more loving than any William had ever known, that kept him by her side.

William IV (formerly the Duke of Clarence), 1831.

Happy ever after?

In 1811 the curse of royal houses everywhere reared its head in Britain: Who would inherit the Crown? There was only one legitimate princess in the next generation, which meant that through no fault, or indeed, wish of his own, the Duke was inching ever-closer to the throne. He now came under pressure to find a young, wealthy and aristocratic bride, and produce legitimate offspring.

After months of agonising, the Duke ended the relationship. Though devastated, Dora never blamed him and, perhaps over-generously, even felt sorry for him in his predicament.

> Do not hear the D of C unfairly abused. He has done wrong, and he is suffering for it.
>
> Letter from Dora to a friend (*c.* 1811)

The separation deal was that their five daughters would stay with her while their five sons lived with the Duke. She would get an allowance and retain custody on one condition: that she never took to the stage again.

It was a generous arrangement but not one that was flexible, and Dora relied too much on the royal family's good nature. When her crooked son-in-law ran up enormous debts in her name, she made the fatal error of going back to work to earn money to pay them off. The Duke promptly ended their arrangement and took everything, including her home, her allowance, and custody of her daughters.

Dora did not live long after this betrayal. She ended her days, as so many had before her, hounded out of the country by creditors. The woman who had supported three families, become one of the most popular actresses of her generation and entranced a prince, died alone in France with none of her children, siblings or friends nearby.

Fifteen years later, when the Duke became William IV, he commissioned a life-size statue of Dora Jordan, showing her cradling a baby with a small child by her knee. The statue was as overlooked after William's death as its subject had been during her life and, after a number of adventures, is now held by the Royal Collections Trust.

ℭimeline

22 November 1761 Dorothea 'Dora' Bland born near Waterford City

21 August 1765 Prince William Henry of Hanover born in Buckingham House (now Palace) to King George III and Queen Charlotte

1785 Dora debuts at Drury Lane as Peggy in *The Country Girl*

1790 Dora and William meet at Drury Lane

1797 Dora and William move to Bushy House, Bushy Park, near Richmond, southwest London (today a scientific institution)

1811 William ends the relationship, remaining in Bushy House with his children

1815 Dora moves to France to avoid arrest for debt

5 July 1816 Dora dies and is buried in the cemetery at Saint-Cloud, near Paris

1818 William marries Adelaide of Saxe-Meinengen; no surviving children

1830 William succeeds his brother George IV as William IV

1831 William IV commissions a marble statue of Dora and two of his children (now in Buckingham Palace)

20 June 1837 William IV dies and is succeeded by his niece Victoria

Actress Dora Jordan, pan pipes and theatrical mask discarded,
shown here as the epitome of maternal love. The marble sculpture was
commissioned from Sir Francis Chantrey (1781–1841) by William IV.

Shakespearean actress Harriet Smithson, 1819.

Painted by Rose Emma Drummond.

Engraved by J. Howard. Jun.r

Miss Harriet Constance Smithson.

Pub. March 1, 1819. by Dean & Munday, Threadneedle Street.

Harriet Smithson & Hector Berlioz

Unhappy woman! If [Harriet] could for one minute conceive the poetry, all the infinitude of my love, she would fly into my arms, though she were to die in my embrace!

Letter from Hector to his friend Ferrand (1830)

One warm night in 1827, the curly-haired, curvy-figured actress Harriet Smithson was going mad onstage at Paris's Odéon Theatre. Watching intently from a box was Hector Berlioz, a struggling musician, and he was entranced.

No one could do insanity and death quite like '*La belle Irlandaise*', as the Parisians dubbed Harriet. Having worked both the Irish and the English theatre circuits for many years, she was now making a speciality of Shakespeare's tragic heroines with Mr Kemble's tour. Her pioneering acting style chimed perfectly with the new fashion in extreme sensitivity, later to be known as the Romantic Movement.

Hector had a 'face like a wounded eagle', as friends described it, unmanageable blond hair and a passionate nature, and he fancied himself a bit of a Romantic hero. At twenty-two, he'd romantically abandoned medical school to concentrate on composing music, much to his parents' annoyance.

Hector couldn't get the vivacious, dark-eyed tragedienne out of his mind. He went to see her again, this time in *Romeo and Juliet*. By the time he emerged into the night, he fancied himself in love.

There's no doubt about it, Hector was obsessive. Despite never having even met the beautiful Harriet, he hung around the stage door, sent flowers and bombarded her with love letters. He couldn't sleep when she was away, and spent nights wandering the streets of Paris pursued by worried friends. He even changed his apartment to one that had a view of her comings and goings to the theatre. He later called this period 'the great drama of my life', and it's fair to wonder: who was he in love with – the real Harriet, her characters, or Love itself?

Nothing is more impossible!
Attributed to Harriet on hearing of Hector's passion

Harriet was blasé when she heard of Hector's obsession; she was at the height of her fame and by now had inspired any number of Romantic poets and artists. Over the next five years, she held Hector at arm's length. In fact, she held him at such arm's length that he found time to become engaged to someone else. However, the young woman's family did not rate Hector and put a stop to it. Hector was becoming an expert in unrequited love.

For five years, Hector continued to be inspired by Harriet, feverishly composing music all the while. In 1832 Harriet attended a performance of his *Symphonie Fantastique*, now considered the world's first great Romantic symphony. This work, which centres on the tale of a suicidal artist's overwhelming but rejected love for a beautiful woman, had obvious autobiographical elements. Weirdly, Harriet wasn't put off by a sequence in which the hero fantasizes about killing his loved one, rather, she was impressed by the passion. Afterwards, she sent a note of congratulations to Hector. They agreed to meet and soon Hector's dream came true; they became lovers.

Their relationship was not without problems. Harriet's French was shaky and Hector's English non-existent, so communication was fraught with misunderstanding. Financially they were in trouble, because Hector was earning very little and Harriet was deeply in debt, having sunk her savings into a theatre venture of her own. In addition, Hector's middle-class family objected to almost everything about Harriet, including the facts that she was poor, Protestant and an actress.

In the year before they married, Harriet herself seemed reluctant to make the journey from mistress to wife – perhaps because she had an inkling that marriage and motherhood would end her career – but Hector was insistent. According to *The Story of Hector Berlioz* by Nathan Haskell Dole, Hector even took poison in Harriet's presence – and then quickly had to take an emetic to make himself throw up. Eventually Fate intervened: as Harriet was planning a benefit performance (an event in which all the proceeds would go to herself), she fell and broke her leg. Hector seized the chance to take care of her. He arranged for fellow-composers Frederic Chopin and Franz Liszt to do a benefit for her, helped pay off her debts and generally made himself indispensable. Harriet capitulated and set the date.

The couple were married at the British Embassy in Paris on 3 October 1833, with Liszt as a witness, and moved into the rue Saint Vincent, Montmartre. The following August, Harriet gave birth to the couple's only child, a boy.

Happy ever after?

After a honeymoon period, their marriage hit trouble; it seems Hector had fallen for Ophelia but then found himself married to Harriet. Just as in *Hamlet*, Ophelia makes the journey from innocent hopefulness to despair, so too did the marriage precipitate Harriet from cautious optimism to drunken disillusionment. Over the next several years, as her husband was unfaithful and absent from home, Harriet became jealous and bitter about his burgeoning career and her own enforced retirement.

In 1841, Hector embarked on an affair with a singer at the Paris Opera. According to Dole, the following year he abandoned his wife, quietly packing his things and leaving her a goodbye note before going on tour to Belgium. In 1844 Harriet moved out of the family home.

Hector Berlioz from an 1878 portrait by Ernst Hader.

While Hector finally got the life he always wanted, Harriet endured hard times. Once their son was at boarding school, Hector no longer supported her financially, and she descended into poverty, moving from one Parisian apartment to another. From 1848, she suffered several strokes, which left her paralysed. She died in 1854 and was buried in the Cimetière Saint-Vincent. Hector chastised himself for his many failings towards her.

Predictably, male contemporaries remembered Harriet only as a muse, not an artist in her own right. 'She inspired you, you loved her, you sang of her, her task was complete,' wrote Liszt of the actress, apparently forgetting that she had revolutionised Shakespearean tragedy before she even met her husband.

Hector had no further luck in matrimony for, although he married his opera-singer mistress, she too died suddenly in 1862. The eccentric composer then decided the most efficient thing to do was to bury both his wives in one place, so he arranged to have Harriet's remains transferred to Montmartre's cemetery, where the rivals were laid to rest together, and where he joined them after his own death.

Timeline —⚬·⚬⟩

18 March 1800 Harriet Smithson born Ennis, County Clare, Ireland

11 December 1803 Louis-Hector Berlioz born La Côte-Saint-André, Isère, France

1814 Harriet debuts at the Theatre Royal, Dublin

1818 Harriet debuts at Drury Lane, London

1827 Hector first sees Harriet onstage at the Odéon, Paris

1830 Hector composes *Symphonie Fantastique*

3 October 1833 Hector and Harriet marry

1834 Louis Berlioz born

1839 Hector composes *Roméo et Juliette*

3 March 1854 Harriet dies 'of paralysis', possibly a stroke, in Paris

1862 Hector removes her remains to his second wife's grave in Montmartre Cemetery, Paris

8 March 1869 Hector dies and is buried with both his wives

Oscar Wilde & Lord Alfred Douglas

I did but touch the honey of romance –
And must I lose a soul's inheritance?

Oscar Wilde, 'Hélas' (1881)

It was tragic, what happened to the witty, wonderful Oscar Wilde, who went from being a leading light to a reviled outcast in a heartbeat. And it all happened because of passion and vengefulness: his passion for Lord Alfred 'Bosie' Douglas, and Bosie's vengefulness towards his hated father.

They met when a mutual friend took Bosie around to see Oscar at his home in Tite Street, Chelsea. At thirty-six years old, Oscar was famous as a playwright and wit. He was also a generous host, a fond (if somewhat bored) husband to his wife, Constance, and a doting father to two children. In the London of the naughty 1890s Oscar danced effortlessly along the edge of raciness, indulging in what polite society deemed outrageous behaviour and getting away with it. He was later known as a man who led a double life.

Bosie was an over-indulged twenty-year-old Oxford dropout

Oscar Wilde, *c.* 1882.

and minor poet. He had tousled blond hair, enormous blue eyes and a toned sportsman's body. As the son of the ninth Marquess of Queensberry, he moved with ease at the very top of society, and included royalty among his pals.

Oscar was a famous aesthete and loved the ancient Greek ideals of beauty and simplicity. He went goggle-eyed at first sight of Bosie, according to the latter's autobiographies, and developed 'an extravagant devotion' to Bosie's physical form, including his rose-red lips and golden hair. After that first meeting, Bosie was treated to lavish lunches, dinners and evenings out, which suited the hard-up lord.

For his part, Bosie claims he found Oscar 'comic-looking' but an extremely entertaining acquaintance. 'Compared with the average man-about-town, he shone,' wrote Bosie in his autobiographical *Oscar Wilde and Myself* (1914), 'and compared with the average "man of genius" he scintillated'.

> I loved [Oscar] because he was brilliant and wonderful and fantastic and fascinating in his mind and in his conversation. His personal appearance, at any rate while I knew him, was always rather against him.
>
> Lord Alfred Douglas, *My Friendship with Oscar Wilde*

Bosie helped Oscar with his translation of his play *Salomé*, and at some point in early 1892 they became lovers (though Bosie would later deny the physical side of their relationship). They appeared everywhere together, and would stay in the best hotels in fashionable

Brighton and Worthing. The relationship featured many break-ups (often about money) and reconciliations. They wrote love letters, some of which ended up in the hands of blackmailers. Meanwhile, Oscar neglected Constance and his children.

Unlike in Europe, homosexual acts between men in Victorian Britain and Ireland were against the law. Being caught meant a prison sentence. Gay and bisexual men, including Oscar and Bosie and their set, had therefore to be discreet about their affairs. Whatever they did in private, they always vehemently denied any accusations of homosexuality in public.

But there was talk, always talk, and Bosie's father, the volatile Marquess, eventually lost patience. He threatened Oscar with a horsewhipping, and attempted to disrupt his smash-hit play *The Importance of Being Ernest*.

One February night in 1895, at the height of Oscar's success, the Marquess approached the Albemarle, a gentleman's club, and left a postcard for all to see emblazoned with the words: 'To Oscar Wilde, posing somdomite [sic].' Despite the weird syntax and creative spelling, it was clear that the Marquess was publicly accusing Oscar of the then-crime of sodomy.

Perhaps Oscar should have ignored it. Perhaps he should have kept his head down and gone on a long holiday. If he had known what was to follow, maybe he would have. After all, Bosie had correctly identified in his 1892 poem, 'Two Loves', that passion between men was 'the love that dare not speak its name'.

But Oscar had been harassed and insulted in public and no true

Lord Alfred Douglas, known as 'Bosie'.

gentleman, gay or straight, was going to tolerate that. With Bosie's encouragement, for his hatred of his father ran deep, Oscar sued the Marquess for libel.

> I really was crazy about the man. The truth is that I really adored him.
>
> *My Friendship with Oscar Wilde*

The trial opened on 3 April 1895 and the Marquess was defended by Edward Carson (later leader of the Ulster Unionist Party). Not only was the case for the prosecution so weak – because it became evident through witness statements that Oscar had not in fact been defamed – but there also emerged so much evidence of Oscar paying for sex with young men that the police were able to charge him with gross indecency.

Friends urged Oscar to save himself by leaving the country. But his own mother, Lady Jane Wilde, insisted that he stay and fight for his good name – and if he didn't, she would never speak to him again. So he waited for the knock on the door and the chance to defend himself. But it was doomed from the outset. After two trials, he was found guilty of gross indecency and, in May 1895, sentenced to the maximum prison sentence of two years' hard labour. Bosie went into exile abroad, and awaited Oscar's release.

Oscar left England for France the same day he was freed, having served all of his sentence. There he changed his name to Sebastian Melmoth and, to the shock of all his friends, joined Bosie in Rouen. This was a short-lived arrangement; the hard years of pain and suffering had chastened Oscar, and he finally saw Bosie for what he was – beautiful only on the outside. They separated, attempted to reconcile once again in Naples, but separated again, this time for good. The following year Oscar's wife Constance died, but he was not allowed to see his children – they had been told he was dead.

> The emotion of the [trial] fanned the waning fires of our devotion to each other ... In the ordinary course of events my infatuation with him would have worn out.
>
> *My Friendship with Oscar Wilde*

Oscar and Bosie met occasionally and remained correspondents until Oscar's death. Oscar spent his last three years eking out a pitiful existence on a £3 per week allowance sent by the aptly named Constance until she died. He lived in increasingly decrepit French hotels and, worst of all, he found he could not write. He died a broken man in Paris at the age of forty-six.

Bosie went on to become rabidly litigious and anti-Semitic. He married, fathered a child and separated from his family. He tried and failed to hold down a job. In a weird symmetry of what happened to Oscar, he spent time in prison for libelling Winston Churchill. It is not clear whether he felt any remorse about the part he played in the downfall of Oscar Wilde.

And all men kill the thing they love,
By all let this be heard,
Some do it with a bitter look,
Some with a flattering word,
The coward does it with a kiss,
The brave man with a sword!

Oscar Wilde, 'The Ballad of Reading Gaol'

Timeline

16 October 1854 Oscar Fingal O'Flahertie Wills Wilde born 21 Westland Row, Dublin, Ireland

22 October 1870 Lord Alfred Bruce Douglas born Powick, Worcestershire, England

1884 Oscar marries Constance Lloyd; they have two sons

1890 Publication of Oscar's only novel, *The Picture of Dorian Gray*

1891 Oscar and Bosie meet

1894 Bosie's poem 'Two Loves' published in the Oxford magazine *The Chameleon*

1895 Oscar stages *The Importance of Being Earnest*

3–5 April 1895 Oscar's libel prosecution against Queensberry fails

26 April 1895 Oscar tried for gross indecency; jury fails to reach a verdict

22 May 1895 Oscar retried for gross indecency; conviction

1897 Oscar released; departs for France

1898 Oscar's 'The Ballad of Reading Gaol' published

7 April 1898 Constance dies

30 November 1900 Oscar dies in Paris, and is temporarily buried in a pauper's grave

1902 Bosie marries Olive Custance; one son

1905 Oscar's *De Profundis* published posthumously

1909 Oscar's supporters have him reburied at Père Lachaise

1924 Bosie serves short prison sentence for libel

1945 Bosie dies, Lancing, Sussex, England

The tomb of Oscar Wilde, designed by Jacob Epstein,
Père Lachaise, Paris.

Love Fast, Die Young

When true hearts lie withered and fond ones are flown
Oh, who would inhabit this bleak world alone?

Thomas Moore, 'The Last Rose of Summer'

From TB epidemics to state-sponsored
executions, when death robs a young couple
of their shared future, one lover must find
the strength to carry on.

Derrynane Abbey, County Kerry, painted in the 1830s.

Eibhlín Dubh Ní Chonaill & Art Ó Laoghaire

I stole away from my kindred with you; I fled from my home
with you. Yet never did I rue that day.
Mrs Morgan John O'Connell (trans),
Old Irish Life at Home and Abroad (1892)

Imagine a bereaved and pregnant young woman, so mad with grief at the death of her husband that she cups the blood pouring from his body to her mouth and drinks it. This is the vivid image at the heart of *Caoineadh Airt Uí Laoghaire* (*Lament for Art O'Leary*), one of the most visceral and personal of all Irish love poems – and it was composed by the widow herself, the poet Eibhlín Dubh Ní Chonaill (Eileen O'Connell).

There is no portrait of Eibhlín Dubh, but we know she had raven hair because 'dubh' (pronounced *dhoov*) means 'black'. Hailing from Derrynane, County Kerry, she was already a widow at twenty-three. At just fifteen years old, she had contracted a dutiful marriage to an elderly man who had obligingly died within the year, leaving Eibhlín free, in her own strong-willed opinion, to find true love.

And find it she did. She spotted the dashing Art Ó Laoghaire (Art O'Leary) from her friend's window one market day as he was riding through Macroom town square. As soon as she clapped eyes on him, she wanted him.

> My love and my delight
> The day I saw you first
> Beside the market house
> I had eyes for nothing else
> And love for none but you.
>
> Frank O'Connor (trans), *A Lament for Art O'Leary*

Proud and grey-eyed, Art was a soldier of fortune, that is, one of the sons of the ancient Catholic houses, who had been dispossessed by the Protestant Ascendancy and forced to leave Ireland to enter military service in the armies of Europe. The bravery of these Wild Geese, as these exiles were known, was legendary.

Art was home on leave from the Austro-Hungarian army. With his beautiful brown mare, given to him by none other than the Empress Maria-Theresa, he cut quite a dash around Cork. He certainly made an impression on Eibhlín. Soon she invited him to Derrynane to meet her father, Dómhnaill Mór Ó Conaill.

Dómhnaill Mór (Big Daniel) had cleverly navigated the diffie cult position of being a Gaelic aristocrat under the Ascendancy boot. He became the Ascendancy's go-to smuggler for brandy and

Kilcrea Abbey, County Cork, c. 1830.

wine, and in return they left him alone to run the territory as the O'Connells saw fit. Despite Art's status and undoubted courage, Dómhnaill Mór and his son, Daniel, had their misgivings about Eibhlín's suitor. In 1773, Daniel wrote that he 'foresaw that [Art's] violence and ungovernable temper would infallibly lead him into misfortune'. In other words, bold Art had a chip on his shoulder and could get the whole clan into trouble.

Dómhnaill Mór therefore refused permission for Eibhlín and Art to marry. Undeterred, the lovers eloped from Derrynane in the middle of the night and, in December 1767, were wed by a Catholic priest in secret. They went to live with Art's father in Rathleigh House, near Macroom.

The couple quickly produced two sons and were blissfully happy. But just as Dómhnaill Mór had feared, Art managed to get up the collective noses of the local bigwigs, causing upset and offence by his behaviour. In particular, he seriously annoyed the magistrate and one-time high sheriff of Cork, Abraham Morris.

For Art was a bit of a show-off. He enjoyed baiting Morris and defying the Penal Laws. For example, he never failed to appear in public in his Hussars uniform, including his famous silver-hilted sword, even though carrying arms was illegal for Catholics in Ireland. In time-honoured tradition, Art also enjoyed bad-mouthing Morris in local taverns.

It is said that the feud came to boiling point when Art's very superior mare beat Morris's horse in a race. The Penal Laws stipulated that no Catholic was permitted to own a horse worth more than £5, and if he did, any Protestant could force a sale for that insulting amount. Morris insisted on invoking the law to buy the animal.

Art, rashly, not only refused to comply but also gave Morris a smack in the face with a horsewhip for his trouble. Morris's retaliation was to persuade his fellow magistrates to have Art decreed an outlaw with a price of twenty guineas on his head. This meant that Art was literally outside the law's protection; anyone could shoot him and claim the reward. He was forced to leave Eibhlín and his children and head for the hills. It is unclear how long Art was in hiding, but it was long enough for him to decide he needed to find Morris and kill him. Unfortunately, news of his plans reached the wrong ears and he was betrayed.

The showdown took place at Carriganimma (*Carraig an Ime* in Irish), nine kilometres south of Millstreet, County Cork. As Art rode along the west bank of the River Foherish, Morris and his men were lying in ambush along the east. Some reports claim that Art, a seasoned soldier, assessed that he was out of range of a musket, and taunted Morris. It was a mistake. A lucky shot from one of Morris's men hit Art in the neck, severing an artery. He clung onto his horse for another few yards, then tumbled to the ground and bled to death.

As soon as she saw Art's riderless, blood-spattered horse galloping towards Rathleigh House, Eibhlín knew her worst nightmare was coming true. She leapt onto the horse and it took her to Art's body. When she got to where Art was lying, she found only an old woman holding vigil, who had charitably covered him with a corner of her cloak. Keening with grief and helplessness, Eibhlín threw herself on his body and scooped his still-warm blood to her lips.

Poetry, in traditional Gaelic society, was often a man's province (though not always – Eibhlín's own mother had been a well-known poet). Keening, however, tended to be a woman's art, and involved one or more mourners producing sustained, rhythmic intoning over a body or grave. Eibhlín was able to combine the two skills:

over the period of her grief, she composed the poem using classical bardic patterns, and she performed it herself. What gives it resonance today is the personal, womanly nature of it, so different from the impersonal recitation of brave deeds and genealogy that a male bard would have produced. One can feel her yearning for the physical presence of her husband, her grief for her fatherless children and her need for vengeance on the murderer.

> I will cross the seas and lay my wrongs before the king,
> If he will not hearken to my tale, I will come back again to
> seek the villain,
> The black-blooded wretch, who tore my loved one from my
> side.
>
> Mrs Morgan John O'Connell, *Old Irish Life at Home and Abroad*

The Lament may have been heard over Art's body several times, for he had three burials. First, Eibhlín arranged his burial at Kilnamartyra, near Dundareirke Castle, County Cork. Then, on the request of the O'Leary family, his body was moved to a temporary grave, before being finally moved to Kilcrea Friary, near Ovens, County Cork, where he rests today under the inscription:

> Lo Arthur Leary, Generous,
> Handsome, Brave, slain in
> His Bloom, Lies in this Humble
> Grave. Died May 4th 1773.
> Aged 26 Years

The Lament was kept alive and recited by local people who knew Eibhlín and Art's tragic story. Some thirty years after the events, a poet heard a beautiful version of it and wrote it down for the first time (in Irish, of course). Many acclaimed poets have produced translations, including Eilís Dillon, Brendan Kennelly, Thomas Kinsella, Frank O'Connor and John Montague.

And as for Eibhlín? Even though she was from a prominent family, even though she was one of the last of the dying order of poets, even though she was the aunt of one of Ireland's most famous figures, Daniel O'Connell, nothing is known of what happened to Eibhlín after she lost her husband. The woman who created a classic funeral poem has no elegy, and lies in an unknown grave.

Timeline

c. 1743 Eibhlín Dubh O'Connell born at Derrynane, County Kerry, one of twenty-two children
1746 Art O'Leary born at Rathleigh House, Macroom, County Cork
1758 Eibhlín marries a Mr O'Connor but is soon widowed
1767 Eibhlín and Art run away to be married
4 May 1773 Art murdered by Morris and his men
7 July 1773 Art's brother Cornelius travels to Cork city and shoots Morris, wounding him
4 September 1773 Magistrates 'honourably acquit' Morris of Art's murder
1775 Morris dies, possibly from complications of the shooting
Early 1800s Eibhlín dies
c. 1800 Nóra Ní Shíndile sings *Caoineadh Airt Uí Laoghaire* (Lament for Art O'Leary) for poet Éamonn de Bhál, who transcribes it for the first time
1940 Frank O'Connor's translation published

Robert Emmet.

PUBLISHED BY HASKELL & ALLEN, 61 HANOVER ST. BOSTON.

ROBERT EMMET.

THE IRISH PATRIOT.

Robert Emmet & Sarah Curran

She is far from the land where her young hero sleeps,

And lovers around her are sighing,

But coldly she turns from their gaze, and weeps,

For her heart in his grave is lying.

Thomas Moore, 'She is far from the land' (1872)

T he story of Robert Emmet and his fiancée Sarah Curran, who were ripped apart by forces beyond their control, is one of the saddest romances in Irish history.

The best likeness of Robert is a miniature sketched during his trial for high treason in 1803. It shows a long nose, a resolute chin and thinning hair combed over his high forehead in Regency fashion. His dark and brooding look – understandable since the man was on trial for his life – belies his idealistic, charismatic, and honourable personality. A few days after this portrait was made, he was executed. He was twenty-five years old.

The likeness of Sarah painted by portraitist William Beechey in 1805 shows a dewy, large-eyed creature, all peaches and cream skin and shiny brown curls. She is also brooding, in this case over her harp, which she caresses lovingly. Three years after this portrait

Sarah too was dead, at twenty-six years old. Neither Robert nor Sarah were survived by children.

Legend has it that the two met and fell in love at a masked ball. But according to a 1904 biography, Sarah and Robert had known each other since childhood because they were part of the same wealthy Anglo-Irish social set, comprising barristers, politicians and landlords. When Robert became best friends with Sarah's brother Richard at Trinity College Dublin, he was invited home to The Priory, Rathfarnham. He developed a rather reverential friendship with the seventeen-year-old Sarah, and she became attracted to his chivalry and sensitive nature. The two exchanged poems.

> [I have] an admiration of the purity of her mind and respect for her talents.
>
> Robert Emmet on his love for Sarah

But Sarah had a controlling father, even by eighteenth-century standards. Prominent barrister, politician and wit John Philpot Curran was apparently so hard to live with that his own wife, Sarah's mother, had absconded with the local vicar. Afterwards his temper kept his daughters under virtual house arrest, and his sons in a permanent state of fight or flight. No courtship was ever going to be easy in the Curran household.

By spring 1798 Robert had become involved with the United Irishmen, a revolutionary group planning an insurrection to overthrow Britain's government in Ireland, then symbolised by Dublin

Castle. Robert's brother, Thomas, was arrested, and Robert had to drop out of Trinity before he was expelled.

You are turning out a rebel on my hands.

This may have been just at the point when the friendship between Sarah and Robert turned to love. It would also explain why the relationship was kept so secret, not just from Mr Curran, who may not have been thrilled at the idea of his daughter being involved with a political hothead and college drop-out, but also from everyone else, including Richard. Robert, fearful of arrest, left Dublin for Paris to gather support for yet another Irish revolution.

They were tempestuous times. The Act of Union of 1800 bound Ireland to Britain and, in many quarters, hopes of a better future withered. But not for Robert. When he returned to Dublin in October 1802, he was no longer a callow student, but a confident man with a plan – and the plan was to replace British rule with a provisional Irish government via a popular uprising. By now leader of the United Irishmen, he set about recruiting men, developing bomb-making factories and stockpiling weapons. He even invented a pike that was hinged and foldable for secrecy. The insurrection was planned for autumn 1803.

He visited Sarah at The Priory when her father wasn't around, and the two became engaged. They talked of their future after the successful rising, about where they would live and how many children they would have.

As a way of trying to protect Sarah, Robert refused to tell her the details of the rising. But she was no fool. Through the autumn of 1802 and the spring of 1803, she knew what was planned, and even advised the over-optimistic Robert in one of her letters not to rely on French reinforcements.

From the start, the 1803 uprising was plagued by rotten luck and poor organisation. A premature explosion forced Robert to change the date, throwing many participants off-balance. Reinforcements from Wicklow did not arrive, nor from France as Sarah had predicted. Men refused to fight because there were not enough weapons. Those who turned out went to the wrong places in fewer numbers.

In Dublin, Robert lost control of his men and a number of revenge killings took place. Robert, in remorse, rejected the rising he had organised. It was over almost before it had begun. Now a wanted man, he went into hiding under an assumed name in Harold's Cross, South Dublin.

Fatally, Robert delayed his escape to France because he was hoping to see Sarah. His safe house was two miles away from The Priory, and Sarah, by now panicking, took to walking there in the hope of catching sight of him. Instead, she watched helplessly as the house was turned upside down by officers of the Crown.

Sarah was beginning to guess that the trouble might extend to herself. Using a go-between, she wrote to Robert, sharing both her fear and faith that their love was strong and could overcome crushed

Sarah Curran Playing the Harp, by William Beechey, 1800.

dreams and failure. And she was careful to tell him to burn her let-ters so they couldn't be traced back to her; it was, after all, a some-what obvious precaution – wasn't it?

It was the letter-writing that did for Robert Emmet in the end. On the evening of 25 August 1803, he was arrested by a Major Sirr and several yeomen, and taken to Kilmainham Gaol. Even though Robert disguised his handwriting, thereby foiling the best attempts of Georgian forensic science, there was still enough of a paper trail to bring him to trial. That was bad enough but, worse still, he had disobeyed Sarah's instructions, and two unsigned letters from her had been found on him.

Robert got into a terrible state about Sarah's letters. He was potentially dragging the woman he adored into a prosecution and ruining her life. Initially refusing to incriminate himself during interrogation, once he found out about the discovery of the letters, he was soon offering to plead guilty and go to the gallows, if only Sarah's name could be suppressed in court.

The offer was rejected because the Attorney General stubbornly refused to believe they were what they were, i.e. love letters, choos-ing to believe instead that they were coded, treasonous messages between collaborators. And, in any case, he had enough evidence to ensure Robert would hang.

Robert decided to write to Sarah one last time. The letter was written in the near-dark of his cell, and in it he tried to allay her fears for her safety, and begged her forgiveness. He entrusted the letter to a warder, George Dunn. For poor Robert, even this last desperate romantic act did not go according to plan. Dunn was an informer and carried the letter straight to Dublin Castle.

> I never felt so oppressed in my life as at the cruel injury I have done you.
>
> Robert's final letter to Sarah

Next morning at breakfast time when Sarah was still in her bed, Major Sirr and his officers came crashing into the house. They raced up the stairs to her room and ransacked it. Sarah became completely hysterical, but her quick-thinking sister, Amelia, grabbed Robert's letters and threw them on the fire.

When Sarah's father returned from business, he hit the roof. He was hearing about his daughter's clandestine goings-on for the first time, the house was in chaos, and his livelihood and reputation were at risk. He now harshly rejected Robert's plea to represent him in court and concentrated instead on smoothing things over with the Castle. Later Robert would write to him expressing how much he was in love with Sarah, and trying to shield her from her father's anger by claiming she never encouraged the relationship. This was to no avail. By the time Robert was writing, Sarah had already been banished from her father's society, exiled to relatives in Cork.

Robert's trial took place on 19 September 1803. He was quickly found guilty and sentenced to be hanged, drawn and quartered as befitted a treasonous crime. Despite the evidence of the burnt scraps and the found letters, which linked Sarah to Robert, if not to the conspiracy, the Attorney General decided not to prosecute her. Instead, the prosecution used extracts from the letters in court without ever naming Sarah. She was safe.

After sentence was pronounced, Robert gave his now-famous and stirring speech from the dock. The following day, he climbed the gallows in Thomas Street, Dublin, to endure a traitor's death. Until the 1880s, when the long drop style of hanging was introduced, those who were hanged did not die quickly from a broken neck but slowly from asphyxiation. Despite this gruesome fate, Robert impressed everyone with unusual calm during his last moments, even helping the hangman to place the noose around his own neck, according to author Patrick Geoghegan. It took thirty minutes to be sure Robert was dead, then he was cut down and his head cut off and held up to the crowd. It is not known where he is buried.

> When my country takes her place among the nations of the earth, then, and not till then, let my epitaph be written.
>
> Robert Emmet, speech from the dock

Happy ever after?

Sarah spent two years in Cork where, it seems, she suffered a breakdown. The recovery was slow but steady, and when she received a marriage proposal from an army surgeon, she accepted. But Fate had not finished with Sarah Curran. Travelling to England from Sicily in the later stages of her first pregnancy, Sarah gave birth prematurely during a ferocious storm. The baby lived only weeks, and Sarah, despairing, died five months later.

Robert and his beloved Sarah have each been immortalised, sympathetically if not entirely accurately, in poetry and song, which include Thomas Moore's 'Oh, breathe not his name' and 'She is far from the land'. Bold Robert is mentioned in the rebel song 'I wish I were back home in Derry', written by Bobby Sands and made famous by Christy Moore. Because of the Emmet brothers' support for American independence, there are monuments to Robert and his brother Thomas in the USA, and Robert is still seen as a hero by the Republican movement.

Timeline

4 March 1778 Robert Emmet born 109 St Stephen's Green, Dublin

1782 Sarah Curran born The Priory, Rathfarnham, Dublin

1798 Robert abruptly leaves Trinity College Dublin and flees to France

1803 Napoleonic War breaks out between Britain and France

23 July 1803 Robert leads rebellion in Dublin

20 September 1803 Robert hanged

1805 Sarah marries Captain Henry Sturgeon

27 December 1807 Sarah gives birth on board a storm-bound ship; the baby dies

5 May 1808 Sarah dies, probably of TB, worsened by pregnancy

1917 Statue of Robert Emmet unveiled in what is now Robert Emmet Park, Washington DC

1919 Statue of Robert Emmet unveiled in Golden Gate Park, San Francisco, for Eamon de Valera's visit during Ireland's War of Independence

1958 Statue of Robert Emmet unveiled in Emmetsburg, Iowa

1968 Statue of Robert Emmet unveiled in St Stephen's Green, Dublin

Charlotte Brontë by George Richmond, 1850.

Charlotte Brontë & Arthur Bell Nicholls

Not that it is a crime to marry, or a crime to wish to be married, but it is an imbecility, which I reject with contempt.

Letter from Charlotte to her dear friend Ellen Nussey (mid-1840s)

In many respects, the touching love story of Charlotte Brontë and Arthur Bell Nicholls resembles some of Charlotte's famous novels – but without the happy endings.

The two met in 1845, when Arthur came from Trinity College Dublin to work for Charlotte's father, the Reverend Patrick Brontë, as his curate. Like his boss who was born and reared in County Down, Arthur was an Ulsterman, hailing originally from Killead, County Antrim. Unlike Brontë, who had very humble origins, Arthur came from a comfortable, property-owning family. Charlotte's father, a gifted scholar, had anglicised his name from Prunty/Brunty to the much posher-looking Brontë while at Cambridge. He was to spend his life seeking to distance himself from his roots and fit in to an English society that looked down on the Irish.

The Parsonage at Haworth, Yorkshire, was full of young

people, who were a similar age to Arthur. The three sisters Brontë and their brother were a tad eccentric – one might even say odd. But Charlotte, Emily, Anne and Branwell were all gifted individuals, whose isolation had served to hothouse their unique talents.

Charlotte was the eldest. At just five feet tall with thick glasses and several missing teeth, she claimed she was so ugly people couldn't look at her for long, and she blamed this for her famous touchiness. She was indeed shy and somewhat waspish, but Charlotte was also strong-spirited, clever and courageous.

Arthur was two or three years younger than Charlotte. He was well built and outdoorsy, and was, according to Charlotte's first biographer Elizabeth Gaskell, 'a grave, reserved, conscientious man with a deep sense of his duties …' He was determined to do well in his first job as a Church of England cleric.

Arthur's responsibility was to teach school, and assist Mr Brontë with the flock of St Michael's and All Angels. And assist he did, mainly with funerals, for Haworth was a particularly unwholesome mill town with a tragically low life expectancy of just twenty-five years.

Charlotte, scribbling away at a table overlooking the ever-expanding graveyard, saw Arthur every day and did not think much of him. Curates ranked low in society, even one who was making himself indispensable. And, unlike many a Victorian miss, Charlotte was in no rush to marry. In her mid-twenties, she had experienced a shocking and unrequited passion for a married Belgian professor, and since then had refused at least two reasonable proposals.

In 1847, Charlotte and her sisters, having admitted to each other they were each secretly writing, published together under men's pseudonyms. Curiously the surname they chose was Bell – part of Arthur's own name. It was an odd choice for such an imaginative bunch, and one wonders what game they were playing. In his novel about Arthur, *The Last Brontë*, SR Whitehead surmises that it was Anne Brontë who attracted Arthur first. Was there rivalry in the parsonage? Some academics maintain that Charlotte was always a mite jealous of Anne, the youngest and prettiest of the sisters.

Charlotte's *Jane Eyre* sold well and made its author famous, an experience that Charlotte hated with a passion. Arthur now had even more reason to keep a respectful distance from the daughters of the house because, as Gaskell says, 'he was not a man to be attracted by literary fame … this by itself would rather repel him when he saw it in possession of a woman.' Not, then, an obvious choice for a successful female writer.

In late 1848 and early 1849, it was Charlotte's sad fate to watch helplessly as the younger Brontës died, one by one, of TB. First, her brother Branwell. Two months later, her beloved Emily. Five months afterwards, Anne.

The Parsonage was now a house of desolation. Charlotte suffered crippling depression, with migraines, insomnia and stomach pain. She was desperately, unremittingly lonely. The reverend leaned heavily on Arthur. The year after losing his children, he commissioned a sanitation report on Haworth, which found that the graveyard by the church was so overcrowded that it was oozing into water sources with deadly results. (Containing up to 42,000 bodies, it finally closed in 1883.)

Between her bouts of illness, Charlotte started to write again. And it was while she was working quietly in her study one December evening that she heard a knock at the door. It was Arthur, shaking and stammering. As soon as she saw him, she knew. He got straight to the point and proposed marriage.

The older, sadder Charlotte did not treat this offer with contempt. Arthur was a good man, and she was so very, very lonely. At thirty-six, this could be her last chance. But her father was furious at the presumption, and chose to see the honest and loyal love of Arthur for Charlotte as treachery against himself. He had lost all his children except one – and he was damned if he was going to let her go. He extracted a promise from Charlotte that she would refuse, which she duly did, believing that the right path for her was the one that required the greatest sacrifice of self-interest. We can only imagine her feelings.

Over the next weeks, the reverend made life so difficult that Arthur resigned. He got a terrific send-off from grateful parishioners, but a stony farewell from Charlotte's father. Loyal Charlotte, bending her strong will to breaking point, passively watched as her lover walked out of her life. Her biographer, Gaskell, admired 'the patient docility which she displayed in her conduct towards her father'.

But Time – and some secret letters between Charlotte and Arthur – did its job. For the next six months, Charlotte worked on the reverend, and eventually he caved in. Arthur was invited back

Arthur Bell Nicholls, *c.* 1854.

to resume his job and live in the parsonage. In due course, he would marry Charlotte. Charlotte, who never expected much pleasure out of her bleak life, experienced a new sensation. It was optimism.

> The destiny which Providence … seems to offer me will not, I am aware, be generally regarded as brilliant, but I trust I see in it some germs of real happiness.
>
> Letter from Charlotte to Miss Wooler (1854)

On Charlotte and Arthur's wedding day the bride was given away by her old schoolteacher, Miss Wooler, because her father could not bear to attend. The couple honeymooned in Dublin, Killarney, Glengariff, Tralee and Cork, then stayed for a month with Arthur's extended family in County Offaly.

Before she married, Charlotte was not enamoured of her own Irish blood, conflicted perhaps by the deep-rooted anti-Irish racism of Victorian Britain levelled against her father. From Ireland she wrote that though she had heard 'a great deal about Irish negligence' she was 'greatly surprised to find so much *English* order and repose in the family habits and arrangements' of her in-laws! Despite her disparagement of the people, her heart was warmed by the welcome she and her husband received.

> My dear husband appears in a new light in his own country, [I hear] his praises on all sides.
>
> Letter from Charlotte to Ellen Nussey (1854)

Her letters to Gaskell from her honeymoon were happy. 'I feel thankful to God for having enabled me to make what seems a right choice ...' she wrote. After their return to Haworth, she reported that 'I have a good, kind attached husband and every day my attachment to him grows stronger.'

Happy ever after?

Like twin spectres, sickness and death still prowled the granite passages of Haworth Parsonage. Charlotte started to suffer symptoms that might have been TB but might also have been the extreme form of morning sickness known as *Hyperemesis gravidarum* (modern famous sufferers have included Kate Middleton). Today women are often hospitalised for the dangerous dehydration and malnourishment that constant vomiting causes, but in Charlotte's day there were no anti-nausea drugs or saline drips.

She lay in bed not eating and barely drinking for six weeks. In a letter to her friend Ellen she confided there was 'No kinder, better husband than mine ... I do not want now for kind companionship in health and the tenderest nursing in sickness.'

It was the last thing she wrote. Just nine months after her wedding, Charlotte died. She was buried in the Brontë vault near the east end of the church where she'd been married.

Arthur loyally continued to assist and care for his father-in-law until the old man's death at the age of eighty-four. He then left the church and went back to farm in Banagher, County Offaly.

The parsonage at Haworth.

There, he married his first cousin Mary Ann Bell; the couple had no children. The man who didn't approve of female writers spent much of the rest of his life controlling access to Charlotte's literary estate and unwillingly managing her growing celebrity.

Timeline

21 April 1816 Charlotte born Thornton, near Bradford, Yorkshire, England

6 January 1819 (or 1818 according to his gravestone) Arthur Bell Nicholls born near Killead, County Antrim, Ireland

1824 Charlotte attends boarding school, where her slight Irish accent is ironed out

1845 Arthur becomes curate to Charlotte's father at Haworth Parsonage

1847 *Jane Eyre* published

1849 *Shirley, A Tale* published

1852 Arthur proposes to Charlotte

1853 *Villette* published

1854 Charlotte and Arthur marry; they honeymoon with Arthur's brother and cousins in Ireland

31 March 1855 Charlotte dies, Haworth, Yorkshire

1864 Arthur remarries

3 December 1906 Arthur dies, Banagher, County Offaly

Grace Gifford Plunkett, 1916.

Grace Gifford & Joseph Plunkett

Darling, darling child, I wish we were together.
Love me always as I love you.
Letter from Joe to Grace, 29 April 1916

Candlelight flickers in a dark prison chapel. The dank walls give off a deathly chill. A young woman gazes into the exhausted face of her man and vows aloud to love him till death parts them. She reaches for him but a soldier grabs her arm and she is steered out of the chapel. Within seconds she is outside in the dark Dublin night.

Such was the midnight wedding of Grace and Joseph 'Joe' Plunkett, who desperately tried to affirm their love for each other against the grim reality of a death sentence.

Grace and Joe probably met around 1910 while moving in the same social and political circles. Appearances were deceptive on both sides. Joe was not as nerdy as he appeared with his high fore-head and round spectacles (or occasionally old-lady pince-nez). He was a poet and newspaper editor, but he was also a fierce sup-porter of Irish independence. He was an important member of the council of the Irish Republican Brotherhood (IRB), the secret organisation that would plan and carry out the Easter Rising.

As for auburn-haired Grace, she may have been quiet and well-spoken, but she was a supporter of the Irish Women's Franchise League and Inghinidhe na hÉireann (Daughters of Ireland), a radical women's organisation, whose activities included forcing local authorities to give meals to poor children. She had no fewer than five sisters, most of whom collaborated with her suffragette and, later, rebel activism.

Joe had admired Grace's subversive caricatures in the feminist paper *The Irish Citizen*, because they punctured fat-cat entitlement with humour. She admired his poetry and fiery prose, which frequently appeared in his republican newspaper, *The Irish Review*, only to be suppressed by the administration in Dublin Castle. In 1915, she started working on the paper as a cartoonist. They became closer when Grace confided to Joe that she wished to become a Catholic.

It is surprising Joe found the time to have a love affair: in 1915 he was keeping so many plates spinning, he was like a variety act. As well as his newspaper and IRB commitments, he spent several months in wartime Germany obtaining guns for the upcoming rebellion, and he visited America. In his leisure time, he studied Arabic, wrote poetry and plays and managed a theatre. Astonishingly, Joe was doing all this while also coping with the serious illness of glandular, or bovine, TB that he had contracted as a child from infected milk, and which was slowly killing him. According to his sister he loved travel, dancing and parties and playing his fiddle. When he had to be quiet due to his illness he hated it. For Joe Plunkett, it was a case

Joseph Mary Plunkett, 1916.

of live fast, die young – one way or the other.

When they announced their engagement in December 1915, there were mixed family reactions. The Plunketts were uber-Catholic (his father was made an honorary Papal Count) and they were nationalists to boot. The Giffords were unionists. The father was Catholic but the mother was Protestant, and they had followed a nineteenth-century custom whereby girls followed their mother's religion and boys followed their father's. They were emphatically not delighted, either on grounds of politics or Joe's ill health.

Joe's letters from around the time of their engagement, housed in the National Library of Ireland, are jokey, passionate and touching. 'I was never meant to be so happy,' he wrote to Grace. 'I love you, I love you, I love you!'

No letters survive from Grace's side of the correspondence, and it's likely that she was having a tougher time of it. When she was baptised a Catholic, her mother all but disowned her, though Joe's delight made up for it. He wrote a poem to celebrate the occasion.

According to Honor Ó Brolcháin, grand-niece of Joseph Plunkett, in her book *All in the Blood: A Memoir of Geraldine Plunkett Dillon*, Grace and Joe became lovers at this time. One of Joe's poems, 'New Love', gives a hint:

> The day I knew you loved me we had lain
> Deep in Coill Doraca down by Gleann na Scath
> Unknown to each till suddenly I saw
> You in the shadow, knew oppressive pain

Stopping my heart, and there you did remain
In dreadful beauty fair without a flaw,
Blinding the eyes that yet could not withdraw
Till wild between us drove the wind and rain.
Breathless we reached the brugh before the west
Burst in full fury—then with lightning stroke
The tempest in my heart roared up and broke
Its barriers, and I swore I would not rest
Till that mad heart was worthy of your breast
Or dead for you—and then this love awoke.

Joseph Plunkett, 'New Love'

A playful letter, partly in Irish, from Joe to his 'heart's delight'.

A SAD ROMANCE OF THE RISING

JOSEPH MARY PLUNKETT
Author of "The Circle and the Sword."

MRS. JOSEPH PLUNKETT,
The original of Mr. W. Orpen's
picture, "Young Ireland."

J. M. Plunkett was one of the Provisional Government and a signatory of the Proclamation of the Republic. In the first hour of Thursday morning, 4th May, Miss Grace Gifford was married to Joseph Mary Plunkett, eldest son of Count and Countess Plunkett. A few hours later the bridegroom was shot in Kilmainham Prison and the young wife became a widow. Every Irish Rebellion has had its love romance, Lord Edward Fitzgerald and Pamela, Robert Emmet and Sarah Curran, Joseph Mary Plunkett and Grace Gifford. Mrs. Joseph Plunkett was born 1888, and is the daughter of a well-known Dublin solicitor. A graduate of the Metropolitan School of Art, she is an excellent black-and-white artist, and has gained distinction as a caricaturist in the Max Beerbohm style, many of her cartoons having been reproduced in "The Irish Review," "The Bystander," and other publications. Her sister, Muriel, was married in 1912 to Thomas MacDonagh, another of the executed leaders.

Iosep O Pluingcéad

Spáid Mic Mic Uilam Naézaip 26

i mbáileáta cliac

Autograph, with address of Joseph Mary Plunkett

Commemorative poster of Joseph Plunkett and Grace Gifford Plunkett, *c.* 1916.

Weddings were different in those days. There was no year-long planning or big white dress or massive party – not for ordinary folks anyway. A couple posted banns to make public their intention. Then they often just slipped into church, with two witnesses, on a morning that suited them and did the deed. During Lent, the six-week run-up to Easter, Joe begged Grace to marry him but, as it wasn't usual to wed during Lent, she wanted to wait for the symbolic date of Easter Sunday. She planned a double wedding alongside Joe's sister Geraldine and her fiancé Tom Dillon. However, Joe had implied that he might be otherwise engaged on that day (i.e. taking part in a revolution), although he wouldn't give details, bound as he was by the secret oath of the IRB.

Just days before Easter weekend Joe underwent surgery to remove tubercular glands from his neck. Grace tended him in the nursing home, where he slept with a gun under his pillow. On the Saturday of Easter weekend, Joe sent Grace what he called 'a little gun' by messenger, and a note to tell her how to use it in self-defence. He discharged himself against medical advice and checked into a Dublin hotel, where he and Grace met for the last time as free people, Joe in full military uniform with bandages and a white silk scarf around his neck.

The Rising was doomed from the start in military terms. After nearly a week occupying the General Post Office and several other sites around Dublin, Joe and his comrades were forced to surrender on 29 April and were marched off to prison to the jeering of the crowd. Joe was housed in Kilmainham. He knew he'd be shot; as a senior officer he had no chance of a reprieve.

On 3 May, Grace received a message. She was to go to the prison to meet Joe and be married there. Sinéad McCoole in *Easter Widows* explains how this unusual act of compassion may have come about. It may have been that, when asked if she 'had to get married' (code for pregnancy), she said she did, and was therefore allowed the ceremony to prevent a possible illegitimate birth.

A veiled and tearful Grace stopped by a jeweller's on the way to buy a ring. She arrived at Kilmainham at about 6pm and waited until 11.30pm before being admitted to the chapel along with a priest, Fr Eugene McCarthy. There she saw Joe, flanked by soldiers with bayonets fixed to their guns. The couple were not permitted to speak to each other except to recite their marriage vows in the presence of Fr McCarthy. (The whole Gifford family were profoundly marked by the events of that week: Grace's sister Nellie was arrested and held in Kilmainham for her role in the Rising as a member of the Irish Citizen Army, and their brother-in-law, Thomas McDonagh, another signatory to the Proclamation, was in a nearby cell awaiting the same fate as Joe.)

After the ceremony, the new Mrs Plunkett went to Fr McCarthy's friend's house nearby and waited. At 2am on 4 May a car arrived, sent by the prison to collect Grace for her last meeting with her husband. It took place in a cell crowded with soldiers and lasted ten minutes.

Joe Plunket was shot by a firing squad before dawn the same day, the youngest of the signatories to die. His wife of less than five hours became his widow for the rest of her life.

Happy ever after?

Grace moved into the Plunkett family home in Kimmage, Dublin, with Geraldine Plunkett Dillon who had married as planned on Easter Sunday. Geraldine claimed that Grace miscarried Joe's baby while she was there. We will never know the truth of this – all we can say is that it was possible, and it might explain why the couple were so desperate to get married.

Unfortunately Grace soon wore out her welcome with the Plunketts, and rows started about money, specifically what she was entitled to as Joe's widow. She wasn't shy about her symbolic value as a widow of a 1916 martyr. Joe had written (in a non-legally binding will) that he wanted 'to give and bequeath everything' to Grace and she eventually threatened his parents with court. They finally agreed to award her £700 from his estate.

Grace became more politically radical after Joe's death. She had a further harrowing experience in 1923, when she was arrested by the Irish Free State for anti-Treaty activities. She spent her husband's seventh anniversary in the same jail where he was executed. She later refused a pension from the government for her role in the founding of the state. When she died in Dublin of heart failure aged sixty-seven, she was given a full military funeral; shots were fired over her grave in Glasnevin.

The tragic wedding of Grace and Joe is one of the many human stories that emerged from the Easter Rising. As news of it spread across the world, it became instrumental in a growth of public support for the Rising and its aims. In 1985, Irish musician Jim McCann, a former member of The Dubliners, recorded 'Grace' – a song written by Sean and Frank O'Meara about the wedding in Kilmainham chapel. This much-loved ballad became a huge hit and is still one of Ireland's most popular love songs.

Timeline

21 November 1887 Joseph Mary Plunkett born at 26 Upper Fitzwilliam Street, Dublin

4 March 1888 Grace Evelyn Gifford born, Rathmines, Dublin

1907 Grace attends Slade School of Art, London

c. 1907 William Orpen paints Grace as 'Young Ireland'

c. 1910 Grace and Joe meet socially

1911 Joe's first volume *The Circle and the Stone* published

1914 Joe and Thomas McDonagh co-found the Irish Theatre Company

1915 Joe attempts raise an Irish Brigade among British soldiers in Germany

11 February 1916 Grace and Joe announce engagement in the press

7 April 1916 Grace baptised a Catholic; Joe presents her with a poem 'For Grace'

4 May 1916 Joe and Grace marry; Joe executed by firing squad, Kilmainham Gaol, Dublin

1917 Grace elected to executive of Sinn Féin

1922 Like the other widows of the Rising, Grace supports anti-Treaty side in Civil War

1923 Grace arrested by the Irish Free State; paints 'The Kilmainham Madonna' on the walls of her cell, which can still be seen today

1932 Fianna Fáil government grants Grace a civil pension

1934 Grace sues Count and Countess Plunkett for support as Joe's widow

13 May 1955 Grace dies of heart failure, Portobello, Dublin and is buried close to the republican plot in Glasnevin Cemetery, Dublin

2016 Frank and Seán O'Meara's 1985 ballad, 'Grace', performed live during RTÉ's Centenary Concert

Bibliography & Sources

PUBLICATIONS

Ashe-Fitzgerald, Mairéad (ed), *Best-Loved Yeats*, The O'Brien Press, Dublin, 2010.

Beckett, Samuel, *Collected Poems*, (eds) Lawlor, Seán, and Pilling, John, Faber & Faber, London, 2013.

Bew, Paul, *Enigma: A New Life of Charles Stewart Parnell*, Gill & Macmillan, Dublin, 2011.

Bingham, Madeleine, *Sheridan: The Track of a Comet*, Unwin Brothers Ltd, London, 1972.

Boaden, James, *The Life of Mrs. Jordan; Including Original Private Correspondence, and Numerous Anecdotes of Her Contemporaries*, Edward Bull, London, 1831.

Bor, Margot, and Clelland, Lamond, *Still the Lark*, Merlin Press, London, 1962.

Brady, Margery, *The Love Story of Parnell and Katherine O'Shea*, Mercier Press, Cork/Dublin, 1991.

Burke, Peter, *Celebrated Trials Connected with the Upper Classes of Society: In the Relations of Private Life*, Benning & Co, London, 1851.

Caldwell, Sir James, *Some authentic particulars of the life of ... J Macnaghton, ... who was executed ..., for the murder of Miss MA Knox*, London and Dublin, 1762.

Churchill, Winston, *Great Contemporaries*, Norton & Co, New York, 1937.

Clare, Anne, *Unlikely Rebels: The Gifford Girls and the Fight for Irish Freedom*, Mercier Press, Cork, 2011.

Daunt, William, *Personal Recollections of the late Daniel O'Connell MP*, Chapman & Hall, London, 1848.

Defoe, Daniel (attrib), *Mother Ross: The life and adventures of Mrs. Christian Davis ...*, London, 1741.

Dent, Alan (ed), *Bernard Shaw and Mrs Patrick Campbell: Their Correspondence*, Gollancz, London, 1952.

Dermot, James, *The Gore-Booths of Lissadell*, The Woodfield Press, Dublin, 2004.

Dillon, Eilís, *The Lament for Arthur O'Leary*, University Review 5, no. 2, 1968.

Dole, Nathan, *A Score of Famous Composers*, TY Crowel & Co, New York, 1891.

Douglas, Lord Alfred, *Oscar Wilde and Myself*, Duffield & Co, New York, 1914.

Douglas, Lord Alfred, *My Friendship with Oscar Wilde*, Coventry House, New York, 1932.

Ellmann, Richard, *Yeats: The Man and the Masks*, Macmillan & Co, London, 1949.

Engels, Friedrich, *The Condition of the Working Class in England*, Blackwell, Oxford, 1971.

Fennell, Conor, *A Little Circle of Kindred Minds: Joyce in Paris*, Green Lamp Editions, Dublin, 2011.

Fitz-Simon, Christopher, *The Boys: A Biography of Micheál MacLíammóir and Hilton Edwards,* Nick Hern Books, London, 1994.

Gaskell, Elizabeth, *The Life of Charlotte Brontë*, Smith, Elder & Co, London, 1858.

Geoghegan, Patrick M, *King Dan: The Rise of Daniel O'Connell 1775–1829*, W&G Baird Ltd, Antrim, 2009.

Geoghegan, Patrick M, *Robert Emmet: A Life*, Gill & Macmillan, Dublin, 2002.

Gilbert, Stuart (ed), *Letters of James Joyce 1882-1941*, Faber & Faber, London, 1957.

Glendinning, Victoria, with Robertson, Judith (eds), *Love's Civil War: Elizabeth Bowen and Charles Ritchie: Letters and diaries, 1941–1973*, Simon & Schuster, London, 2009.

Gore-Booth, Eva, *Poems of Eva Gore-Booth, with the Inner Life of a Child and Letters and a Biographical Introduction* by Esther Roper, Longmans & Co, London, 1929.

Gregory, Lady Augusta, *Cuchulain of Muirthemne: The story of the men of the Red Branch of Ulster*, John Murray, London, 1902.

Hutton, Mary A (ed), *The Táin: An Irish Epic Told in English Verse*, Talbot Press, Dublin, 1924.

Kehoe, Elisabeth, *Ireland's Misfortune: The Turbulent Life of Kitty O'Shea*, Atlantic Books, London, 2008.

Knowlson, James, *Damned to Fame: The Life of Samuel Beckett*, Bloomsbury Publishing, London, 1997.

MacDonagh, Oliver, *The Life of Daniel O'Connell 1775–1847*, Weidenfeld & Nicolson, London, 1991.

MacManus, Seumas (ed) *Poems by 'Eva' of The Nation (Mary Eva Kelly)*, MH Gill & Son, Dublin, 1909.

McCoole, Sinéad, *Easter Widows*, Doubleday Ireland and Transworld Digital, London, 2014.

McCoole, Sinéad, *No Ordinary Women*, The O'Brien Press, Dublin, 2015.

Mac Liammóir, Micheál, *All for Hecuba: An Irish Theatrical Autobiography*,

Methuen & Co, London, 1946.

Masefield, John, *John M. Synge: A few personal recollections*, Folcroft Library Editions, 1977.

Massey, Eithne, *Legendary Ireland*, The O'Brien Press, Dublin, 2013.

Mavor, Elizabeth, *Ladies of Llangollen: A Study in Romantic Friendship*, Penguin, London, 1973.

Mitchel, John, *Jail Journal*, University Press of Ireland, 1982.

Murphy, Allison, *Winnie & George: An Unlikely Union*, Mercier Press, Cork, 2017.

Ó Broin, León (ed), *In Great Haste: The letters of Michael Collins and Kitty Kiernan*, Gill & MacMillan, Dublin, 1983.

Ó Brolcháin, Honor, *16 Lives: Joseph Plunkett*, The O'Brien Press, Dublin, 2012.

O'Casey, Eileen, *Sean*, Macmillan & Co, London, 1971.

O'Casey, Sean, *Rose and Crown*, Macmillan & Co, London, 1952.

O'Connell, Morgan John, *The Last Colonel of the Irish Brigade: Count O'Connell and Old Irish Life at Home and Abroad, 1745–1833*, Kegan Paul & Co, London, 1892.

O'Connor, Frank (trans), *A Lament for Art O'Leary*, Cuala Press, Dublin, 1940.

O'Doherty, EM, *Poems by 'Eva' of The Nation*, MT Gill, Dublin, 1909.

O'Shea, Katharine, *Charles Stewart Parnell: His Love Story and Political Life (2 vols)*, Cassell & Co Ltd, London, 1914 & 1921.

Parton, James, *Life of Andrew Jackson*, Mason Brothers, New York, 1860.

Patrick, Ross, and Patrick, Heather, *Exiles Undaunted: The Irish rebels, Kevin and Eva O'Doherty*, University of Queensland Press, 1989.

Peters, Margot, *Mrs Pat: The Life of Mrs. Patrick Campbell*, Hamilton, London, 1985.

Plunkett, Joseph, *The Poems of Joseph Mary Plunkett* (fourth ed), Talbot Press, Dublin, 1919.

Russell, Jane, *James Starkey/Seumas O'Sullivan: A critical biography*, Associated University Presses, 1987.

Ryan, Meda, *Michael Collins and the Women Who Spied for Ireland*, Mercier Press, Cork/Dublin, 2006.

Saddlemyer, Ann (ed) *Letters to Molly, John Millington Synge to Máire O'Neill, 1906–1909*, OUP, London, 1971.

Sirr, Harry, *Sarah Curran's and Robert Emmet's Letters*, MS Notes, Hodges, Figgis & Co, Dublin, 1910.

Tomalin, Claire, *Mrs Jordan's Profession: The Actress and the Prince*, Penguin, London, 1995.

Walshe, Éibhear (ed), *Sex, Nation and Dissent in Irish Writing*, Cork University Press, Cork, 1997.

Whitfield, Roy, *Friedrich Engels in Manchester: The Search for a Shadow*, Working Class Movement Library, Manchester, 1988.

Yeats WB, *Synge and the Ireland of his Time*, Cuala Press, Dublin, 1911.

ARTICLES

Kennedy, Michael, 'The Life and Times of Half-Hanged McNaghten 1724–61', Strabane Historical Society, 2016.

Novak, Rose, 'Reviving "Eva" of The Nation: Eva O'Doherty's Young Ireland Newspaper Poetry', in *JSTOR*, www.jstor.org/stable/43663146, accessed 20 November 2020.

Peters, Margot, 'Bernard Shaw and Stella Pat' in *Biography*, vol. 9, no. 1, 1986, pp. 25–36, *JSTOR*, www.jstor.org/stable/23539285, accessed 17 April 2020.

ONLINE SOURCES

www.aughty.org

www.ballingearyhs.com

www.bangorhistoricalsocietyni.org

www.bbc.co.uk

www.bl.uk

www.bronte.org.uk

https://chroniclingamerica.loc.gov

www.dctrust.ie

https://dib.cambridge.org

http://doras.dcu.ie

www.duchas.ie

www.durrushistory.com

http://enniscorthyathenaeum.com

www.firstladies.org

https://georgianera.wordpress.com

www.glasnevintrust.ie

www.historyireland.com

http://ianpindar.blogspot.com

www.irelandsown.ie

www.irishcentral.com

www.irishhistorian.com

www.irishmeninparis.org

www.irishtimes.com

http://kiernanfamily.wordpress.com

www.liffordoldcourthouse.com

www.lisburn.com

www.maritaconlonmckenna.com

www.millstreet.ie

http://mspcsearch.militaryarchives.ie

www.oxforddnb.com

https://strabanehistorysociety.org

www.theguardian.com

www.thehermitage.com

www.theheroinecollective.com

www.theirishstory.com

www.tribunemag.co.uk

Picture Credits

The author and publisher would like to thank the following for permission to reproduce photographs and illustrative material:

Front cover image: Jean Reutlinger (1875–1917) Wikimedia Commons; Back cover image: Library of Congress; Internal images: p80 Agefotostock.com; pp 18, 26, 29, 68 Alamy; p263 Courtesy of the Brontë Society and Brontë Parsonage Museum; p253 Reproduced courtesy of Calderdale Metropolitan Borough Council; p89 ESB Centre for the Study of Irish Art collection. Image © National Gallery of Ireland; pp271, 273 Honor Ó Brolcháin; p203 JFK Library; pp52, 55 John Oxley Library/State Library of Queensland; p120 Independent News & Media; pp92 (KMGLM.2012.0243), 274 (KMGLM.17NO-1I51-03) Courtesy of Kilmainham Gaol Museum/OPW; pp33, 34, 37, 40, 98, 158, 166 (both), 172, 188, 227, 240, 248, 258 Library of Congress; pp44, 117 (© The March of the Women Collection), 138, 162, 180, 200 Courtesy of Mary Evans Picture Library; pp8-9 Richard Mills; pp60, 63, 66-7, 108, 128, 147, 152-3, 195, 214, 222, 268 Courtesy of the National Library of Ireland; p175 The Office of Public Works; p144 Pip Sides/The O'Brien Press; p221 Royal Collection Trust/© Her Majesty Queen Elizabeth II 2021; pp42-3, 48, 72-3, 78-9, 106-7, 114, 126-7, 135, 156-7, 184-5, 206-7, 208, 218, 237, 238-9, 266 Shutterstock; p21 UB James Joyce Collection, courtesy of the Poetry Collection of the University Libraries, University at Buffalo, The State University of New York; pp5, 10, 15, 103, 230, 233, 243 WikiCommons.

Text credits

The author and publisher would like to thank the following for permission to reproduce quotations from:

Beckett, Samuel, 'Cascando' in *Poems in English*, John Calder Ltd, London, 1961.

Beckett, Samuel, *Poems in English and French*, Grove Atlantic, London, 1977.

Glendinning, Victoria with Robertson, Judith (eds), *Love's Civil War: Elizabeth Bowen and Charles Ritchie*, Simon & Schuster, London, 2009. By kind permission of David Higham Associates.

Gonne, Maud, *A Servant of the Queen: Reminiscences*, University of Chicago Press, 1938.

'The Legend of Lough Sheelin' © National Folklore Collection, UCD.

The author and publishers have endeavoured to establish the origin of all in copyright images and quotations used. If any involuntary infringement of copyright has occurred, sincere apologies are offered, and the owners of such copyright are requested to contact the publisher.

Also by Marian Broderick

'Broderick's fascination with her two favourite subjects – Irish history and women's studies – jumps out from every page'
Sunday Business Post

In times when women were expected to marry and have children, they travelled the world and sought out adventures; in times when women were expected to be seen and not heard, they spoke out in loud voices against oppression; in times when women were expected to have no interest in politics, literature, art, or the outside world, they used every creative means available to give expression to their thoughts, ideas and beliefs.

In a series of succinct and often amusing biographies, Marian Broderick tells the life stories of these exceptional Irish women.